Easy Access (For The Boys)
&
All Over Lovely

Two plays from 'the female counterpart to Quentin Crisp'
Evening Standard

Easy Access (For The Boys)
Michael – a young prostitute – is making a video diary. He and
his friend Gary were both sexually abused by their fathers. Gary
can't believe that Michael gets on well with his dad. 'Let's go
over – one last time – and beat the crap out of him.'

All Over Lovely
'Dowie's gimlet-eyed script digs deep, then deeper, into the
questions it raises, refusing glib answers as it unpicks constructions
such as beauty, gender conditioning, political correctness, sisterly
and sexual love ... A show as stimulating as it is entertaining.'
Scotsman

Claire Dowie is a writer/performer/poet/comedian and pioneer
of what she calls 'stand-up theatre'. She started out writing and
performing poetry on the original so-called 'alternative' comedy
circuit in London, then switched to stand-up comedy and started
writing plays 'when the punchlines ran out'. Her first play *Cat and
Mouse* was performed in 1987, followed by *Adult Child/Dead Child*
(1988, *Time Out* Award), *Why Is John Lennon Wearing A Skirt?* (1991,
London Fringe Award), *Death and Dancing, Drag Act, Leaking from
Every Orifice* (all published by Methuen) and *All Over Lovely*. She was
awarded an Arts Council bursary in 1995 to write *Easy Access (For
the Boys)*, a play without a part in it for her. Other work includes
Came Out, It Rained, Went back In Again (1992, BBC2, part of City
Shorts season); *Kevin* (1994, Central Children's Television); *The Year
of the Monkey* (1995, BBC Radio Three). She has recently
completed a second commission for BBC Radio, *From the Bottom of
a Well*.

by the same author

**Why Is John Lennon Wearing A Skirt?
and other stand-up theatre plays**

Claire Dowie

Easy Access (For The Boys)
&
All Over Lovely

BLOOMSBURY

LONDON • NEW DELHI • NEW YORK • SYDNEY

Bloomsbury Methuen Drama
An imprint of Bloomsbury Publishing Plc

50 Bedford Square   1385 Broadway
London   New York
WC1B 3DP   NY 10018
UK   USA

www.bloomsbury.com

Bloomsbury is a registered trade mark of Bloomsbury Publishing Plc

First published 1998 by Methuen

Visit www.bloomsbury.com to find out more about our authors and their books
You will find extracts, author interviews, author events and you can sign up for
newsletters to be the first to hear about our latest releases and special offers.

British Library Cataloguing-in-Publication Data
A catalogue record for this book is available from the British Library.

ISBN: PB: 978-0-4137-1290-5
EPDF: 978-1-4081-5513-4
EPUB: 978-1-4725-3797-3

Library of Congress Cataloging-in-Publication Data
A catalog record for this book is available from the Library of Congress.

Contents

Easy Access (For The Boys)

Easy Access (For The Boys) was first performed at the Drill Hall, London, on 30 January 1998. The cast was as follows:

Michael	Jud Charlton
Gary	Nicholas Bailey
Ed	Peter Marinker
Matt	Malcolm James
Ruth	Natasha Langridge

Directed by Claire Dowie

Onstage.

Michael *and* **Gary** *watching the video, and taking the piss.*

Video.

External. The 'meat rack'. **Gary** *'operating' the camera.* **Michael** *dressed very young and sexily, perched on a safety railing, surveying his surroundings to begin with but then turning to smile into the camera:*

Michael   This is where I started, on the meat rack. Where we met up in actual fact – my friend Gary the cameraman. It's quite simple, all you do is . . . oh hang on, Gary, my luck's in . . .

Michael *jumps off the railing and disappears.*

Gary (*calling after him*)   Michael! Michael!

Cut to: **Gary** *'operating' the camera.* **Michael** *standing outside a shop, showing postcard notices in the window, dressed older, but still sexy.*

Michael   I then progressed to a card, in this shop window 'Michael. Young, male masseur.' And then my phone number.

He grins cheekily. **Gary** *snorts a laugh from behind the camera.*

And from postcards to . . .

He holds up a mobile phone.

Real style.

Cut to: Internal. **Ed***'s café/bar.* **Ed** *sitting, being interviewed by* **Michael** (*interviewer*), *pretending* **Michael** *is a proper interviewer.*

Ed   My son, he's a rent boy. Or rather I should say male prostitute, doesn't like being called a rent boy any more, says he's too old – and organised. I see him from time to time, we have a good relationship, better than most fathers and sons I think, I hope. Certainly better than I had with my dad anyway. I don't know too much about what goes on but I think he must be fairly successful because he always seems to have money – he's certainly got more money than I've ever had. Erm . . . what else?

Michael (*interviewer*) How do you feel about it?

Ed How do I feel? About him being a rent boy? Erm . . . I don't actually know too much about it, other than what he's told me, and that sounds pretty boring for the most part. Sounds like just a job really. I certainly don't feel morally judgemental or anything. He's paranoid about using condoms so I don't worry about Aids particularly, I mean he's very sensible. Other than that and the occasional worrying incident . . .

Onstage.

Gary Worrying incident?

Michael Shhh.

Video.

Ed Which is like er . . . hazard of the job I suppose, I don't think it's half as bad as people would have us believe.

Michael (*interviewer*) But surely 'worrying incidents' and 'hazards of the job' are the very reasons why most fathers don't have aspirations for their sons to become whores.

Onstage, **Gary** *laughs.*

Ed I don't aspire to you becoming a whore, Michael?

Michael (*interviewer*) Well, whatever the word, get on with it.

Ed No, because you're making out like I don't care what you do, or I pushed you into it or something, which couldn't be further from the truth.

Onstage.

Gary Uh huh.

Michael   What do you mean 'uh huh'?

Video.

Michael (*interviewer*)   Yeah I know, I know, come on, this is supposed to be a proper interview.

Ed   Well, get your words right then.

Onstage.

Gary   Didn't push you into it.

Michael   He didn't.

Video.

Michael (*interviewer*)   Well, whatever the word is – why most fathers don't . . .

Onstage.

Gary   Whether you're fucked with a smile or fucked with a sneer you're still getting fucked.

Michael   Fuck off, Gary.

Video.

Ed   I don't 'worry' about the possible hazards as much perhaps as some parents because, as my son's pointed out, a tube driver is a respectable job, a bank manager is a respectable job, but the tube driver had a suicide throw themselves in front of his train and the bank manager had a sawn-off shotgun stuck in his face. Both men had to quit their jobs. My son's been beaten up a couple of times, assaulted, but nothing so deeply traumatising that he quit his job – so whose job's worse?

Onstage.

Gary   I've had that tube driver.

Michael   Who hasn't.

Video.

Michael (*interviewer*)   So your point is?

Ed   My point – or rather my son's point, is that life's pretty hazardous anyway and so long as you take care and know what you're doing ... and according to him most punters are really quite sweet.

Onstage.

Gary   Yeah, sweet – like cyanide.

Video.

Ed   So I might not necessarily like what he does but – there are worse jobs.

Michael (*interviewer*)   Such as what?

Onstage.

Gary   Being you for one thing.

Michael   Gary.

Video.

Ed   I don't know, mass murderer? Prime minister?

Onstage.

Gary   Well, I hate your dad, he's a wanker.

Video.

Michael (*interviewer*)   Be serious.

Onstage.

Michael   And yours isn't?

Video.

Ed   I don't know, any job that drives you nuts I suppose. I can't think of anything else to say.

Onstage.

Gary   At least he's not a hypocrite.

Michael   No, too busy being a fucking maniac.

Gary   Yeah. Which we all acknowledge, which we all accept. At least I don't waste my time pissing around pretending my dad's good, pretending my dad's OK. At least I'm realistic.

Video.

Michael (*interviewer*)   So you think sucking for success is a good job?

Ed   I thought you said you wanted to do a serious interview?

Michael (*interviewer*) *laughs.*

Onstage.

Michael *turns the video off.*

Michael   What? What was wrong with that? (*Gesturing to the video.*) What's wrong with having a dad who's supportive, who you can visit and get on with, and who cares about you? What's wrong with forgiving and forgetting?

Gary   Because you can't and you won't, and you're an arsehole to try. Because you're just burying it, and if you really think your dad's good, then you must think nothing of yourself, you must have absolutely no self-esteem whatsoever, and your dad might as well be a pimp. In fact he is one really, when you get down to it. He's a fucking pimp who couldn't give two shits about you, and just so long as you don't rock the boat he's going to carry on smiling.

Michael   God, you don't half talk a load of bollocks sometimes!

Gary Yeah well at least I don't think it.

Michael Meaning? Meaning?

Gary Nothing. Forget it. Look what are we arguing for? Huh? I don't like your dad, never have done, so what do you want me to say?

Michael Nothing.

Gary Right then, I'll say nothing.

Michael *talking to audience (recording video diary).*

Michael Apparently, if you've put up with so-called sexual abuse, then you have to automatically hate the abuser. 'Put up with', 'abuse'. I never put up with anything, I never felt abused. And I certainly don't hate anyone. I get on well with my dad and I'd like to keep it that way, and if that means not talking about certain ... events, then so be it. I'd hate us to fall out over something as ... meaningless as sex. Although I know some would regard child sex as anything but meaningless but ... that's their problem, I don't suffer from it. Gary's just trying to make me. He's determined to turn what happened into something that it wasn't. Gary had a horrible life, I think his dad was a real psycho. I can't imagine what it was like for him, really shitty. He's my best friend, but I hate the way he thinks my dad is automatically the same as his. I love my dad actually. Sometimes it makes me want to punch him. Gary I mean, not my dad.

Video diary.

Michael *talking live with simultaneous video projection.*

Michael When I was about thirteen, I lay awake night after night for months, don't know how many, listening to every creak, every noise, waiting. I'd be angry in the evenings, blast music or television, try to bury the music from downstairs, the customers, the ... jollity. The atmosphere, couldn't bear the atmosphere, crowded café downstairs, people laughing, drinking, talking, music playing, me upstairs, alone, out of it, waiting. Even now, if neighbours play music, have a party or something, I have to get out, go to a bar, mix with people, meet people. I spend most of my life in bars, love bars – crowded, noisy, drunken bars, get myself in the midst of it, try to blot out the idea that someone is close, upstairs, alone, overhearing, maybe waiting, somebody else maybe waiting. Not me though, it's never again going to be me. If there's a punter then I beat the image, the bar's just a bar, no surroundings, no upstairs, I'm in control – not drunk, I never get drunk when I'm working, a couple to loosen up but never drunk, I want to be in control of this guy. But if there's not a punter, if I can't hack a punter sometimes, and sometimes I just can't, sometimes I just don't want to know, then I'll go someplace else. I try to relax, give myself a night off, but without a punter, without even the idea of a punter, well there's only alcohol then. Alcohol and loud music and dancing – and perhaps a quick blowjob in the toilets with a stranger – just for the heck of it.

Onstage.

Matt I've been watching you, I hope you don't mind. It's nice to see someone in my bed for a change, makes the bedroom seem more interesting. I'd thought about redecorating but obviously all it needed was another body.

Michael What went on last night?

Matt You looked really peaceful, young. Mind you, you look haggard now. It's amazing how quickly your face changed.

Michael What did we do? Did we do anything?

Matt Still, it's a relief to see you're not as young as I'd worried you might be.

Michael Did we fuck or what?

Matt Not old though, still chicken enough for me. Bet you're incredibly hung over. It's none of my business of course, but if you ask me you drink far too much.

Michael Oh fuck off, will you, I don't need lectures right now. So what happened?

Matt About what?

Michael Last night? What happened last night?

Matt You were totally out of it, that's what happened, tanked up to the gills.

Michael What did we do?

Matt I expect you want some coffee, here put this on.

Michael Did we fuck or what?

Michael *looks at it: a hooded, towelling dressing-gown.*

Matt As worn by the young noviciate monks of Reculver Castle.

Michael *raises his eyebrows.* **Matt** *disappears.* **Michael** *looks at the dressing-gown, puts it on.*

Michael (*calling*) Should I put the hood up or down?

No answer. **Michael** *tries it both ways. Waits. Music fades up slowly.* **Ed** *starts closing up the bar, clearing the ashtrays, collecting and washing glasses, takes his time.* **Michael** *waiting.* **Ed** *checks the till, checks the bar, wipes surfaces etc., finally turns off music.* **Michael** *waits, still, but getting sexually aroused.* **Ed**, *one final check around the place, turns off lights, leaves on stair light (semi gloom).* **Michael** *waiting, listening. Silence apart from occasional creaks in the semi gloom. Finally door opens, light spills in,* **Michael** *heightened tension, sexual expectation.* **Matt** *bangs on the light.*

Matt Coffee.

Michael *looks sharply at* **Matt**.

Michael What?

Matt Coffee.

Gary Straight gays, they haven't a clue. I don't know

why you waste your time. Oh fine for a while, a novelty even, but come on, Michael, they're living in a different world. And anyway have you ever stopped to consider what he's getting out of it? Why's he interested? Does he get his kicks fucking slags for free?

Michael You're jealous.

Gary What?

Michael You're jealous.

Gary Of having a boyfriend? A so-called fine, upstanding member of the nine to five, toe the line, loving relationships just like straights, gay community?

Michael Yes.

Gary Michael, I have had boyfriends before, and felt murderous for weeks after they've dumped me because the novelty wore off and the fear of disease wore on. They think you're exciting, they get their kicks out of hearing tales of your exploits, they know you'll do ANYTHING to please them. Then they get fed up trying to cover up who you are and what you do to their friends – how does Matt explain you to his friends? How do you explain yourself?

Michael Outreach worker for the homeless.

Michael *and* **Gary** *both laugh.*

Gary Whoo that's a good one, must remember to use that one myself sometime. See what I'm saying?

Matt You dreamed that one up not me. I'm not ashamed of what or who you are. I'd be quite happy to be honest with people. It's you I care about not them. Of course we have to be a little bit guarded with Jackie, but we both agreed, that's nothing against you, that's just about access to Becky, I mean God, I'm guarded, I was guarded before I even met you, as you well know.

Michael *talking to audience.*

Michael Matt I trust, I think. Well, sometimes I do.

Sometimes I don't obviously. But basically I think I trust him more times than I don't, so I suppose he's trustworthy. Basically. And I think Matt trusts me. He sort of accepts what I do, although we have the occasional argument about it but ... I haven't told him about my dad, yet. I'm going to, I think it's necessary but ... I suppose I'm waiting for the right time. No I'm not actually, to be honest I'm scared to death of telling him, I don't want to tell him. A lot of people, straight people, they go on about cycles of abuse and how abusers were once abused and ... abuse breeding abuse breeding abuse and I wasn't abused, I know I wasn't abused but try telling that to people? Try telling them it's OK, no worries, I LIKE my dad. Try telling them I don't feel abused, I don't feel abusive, but then see how suspicious they become. So I don't know what he'd think and ... I want him to want me. I like being with him. And little Becky. And he doesn't touch her at all, doesn't do anything, doesn't even cross his mind. I thought that was weird at first, I kept looking for signs, kept thinking oh he must be, why else would he want access? But he doesn't, he just loves her – normally. Had so much respect for him then. I suppose having Becky attracted me to him even more. Because I want to understand that, I want to be a part of something where sex isn't always at the heart of everything. Because to be honest I am so sick of sex, so ... fed up with the cynicism of my friends and the pathetic maulings and manouverings of punters. I'm getting old, getting too old for this game, I want something else.

Matt *massaging* **Michael**'*s shoulders, kissing his neck, etc.*

Matt   You must be tired.

Michael   Umm.

Matt   Becky's coming tomorrow.

Michael   Good. We can take her to Margate.

Matt   You're obsessed with Margate.

Michael   She loves it there.

Matt You love it there. Don't know how you've got the
gall to go on all those kiddy rides with your knees round
your ears.

Michael I'm used to having my knees round my ears.

Matt Humm I'll bet you are. So how many rides have
you been on today, little boy? Completely knackered or
room for a little one inside?

Michael Completely knackered.

Matt Shame, because she's coming for the weekend so
I'll need two days of making use of you squeezed into the
next hour or so. How tired?

Michael Very tired.

Matt Too tired to put up a fight?

Michael Maybe a bit of a fight.

Matt Good, I like a bit of resistance, would hate to think
any Tom, Dick or Harry could just spunk all over you. I
assume you've already showered . . .

Matt *undoing* **Michael**'*s shirt etc.* **Michael** *very still, passive.*
Michael *getting more aroused (though still passive) as* **Ed** *joins*
Matt *in rubbing, massaging, kissing etc.* **Michael**'*s body. But as*
Matt *backs off and* **Ed** *takes over completely,* **Michael** *becomes*
active and reciprocates to **Matt**, **Ed** *then backs off, 'fades away'.*

Gary Has he introduced you to the folks yet? Have you
taken tea with mumsy?

Matt Oh come on, Michael, you know full well my
parents live in Edinburgh, Christ, I hardly get to see them
myself. Plus the fact that I invited you to come with us that
time but I seem to recall you were otherwise engaged with
a very rich American who you were skinning alive on his
two-week vacation around 'quaint little old London'.

Gary Which came first, the idea of the visit or the rich
American jam pot?

Matt God, how long does this suspicion and mistrust

have to go on? If I didn't want you I wouldn't be here.

Gary   What does he want you for?

Michael *talking to audience.*

Michael   There wasn't an American, I made him up. I don't know why. I mean the idea of spending a weekend with Matt and Becky was ... well, I'd have loved to. I don't get to sleep at Matt's when Becky's there in case she comes charging into the bedroom or something so ... Edinburgh for a weekend, a whole weekend, but with his parents as well? So hey presto, suddenly I'm dining at the Dorch every night. Everybody was terribly impressed. Including Matt. I suppose I'm just not into meeting people's mothers. I mean God knows I have a hard enough time with my own.

Video.

Internal. **Ed**'s café/bar. **Ed** *standing behind bar.*

Ed   It's my fault really. Looking back I suppose I was pretty selfish but (*Gesturing.*) I wanted this place so badly. I mean look at it, it's all I ever wanted. I didn't care that we had no other money, I don't care about working all hours – I like working all hours, and OK so the profit margin's negligible, but it's mine and I can do what I like, and nobody, nobody, can tell me what to do. And your mum, well, I suppose it just wasn't your mum's dream, nobody's fault really.

Onstage.

Gary   It's funny how you bang on endlessly about your dad, but never mention your mum.

Matt   I think possibly, deep down, and you might not like me saying this but, have you ever thought that a lot of your problems stem from what your mother did?

Michael *talking to video camera and/or audience.*

Michael   Not that there's anything wrong with my

mother, we've just . . . grown apart, that's all.

Video.

Internal. **Michael**'s **Mum**'s *house.* **Mum** *arguing at the camera* (**Michael**).

Mum   Have you any idea what it's like to have no home, no job, no money, nowhere to go? What did you expect me to do? Live in a crummy bed-sit with a six-year-old? How was I supposed to get a job then? Bad enough that my only talent seems to be quoting Bob Dylan lyrics endlessly, which is weird because I didn't even like Bob Dylan till I met your dad. I swear he twisted me, you know . . . Bad enough that I wasted a lot of years trying to get as enthusiastic about the café as your dad was, without the qualifications that he had, so that should I want to get a job in a similar vein, which I didn't, because that's why I left, I could be a waitress or a barmaid – big deal! Mega bucks! Oh give me a mortgage and make it a big one! And you think I should start from scratch with nothing, knowing nothing, with a six-year-old! Grow up, Michael!

Onstage. **Michael** *talking to audience.*

Michael   Oh I understand it. I understand it all too well, every time we have an argument it crops up. I don't want it to, it just always comes out, eventually. She says it's about time I grew up, and I agree really. I mean I am grown up, I do understand . . . but it still makes me rage, makes me argue. I get so irritated with myself, I always end up slamming out, calling her a bitch and worse, and thinking why am I harking on this old stuff all the time, why can't I get over it? (*To* **Matt**.) What do you mean 'what my mother did'? She didn't do anything!

Matt   She walked out.

Michael   She divorced my dad.

Matt   Walked out without you.

Michael   Have you any idea what it's like to have no

home, no job, no money, nowhere to go? What did you expect her to do? Live in a crummy bed-sit with a six-year-old? How was she supposed to get a job then? Bad enough that her only talent seems to be quoting Bob Dylan lyrics endlessly, which is weird because she didn't even like Bob Dylan till she met my dad. She says he twisted her – but that's pathetic. Bad enough that she wasted a lot of years trying to get as enthusiastic about the café as dad was, without the qualifications that he had, so that should she want to get a job in a similar vein, which she didn't, because that's why she left, she could be a waitress or a barmaid – big deal! Mega bucks! Oh give me a mortgage and make it a big one! And you think she should start from scratch with nothing, knowing nothing, with a six-year-old! Grow up, Matt!

Matt   Other women have managed it.

Michael   Oh shut up. It's true. It's understandable.

Matt   Jackie's managed.

Michael   Jackie's got a bloody good job, and so have you. You might complain about alimony but I don't see you suffering. And besides which it's more fashionable now, my mum obviously had a harder time.

Matt   What's more fashionable?

Michael   Single parent career woman.

Matt   Are you saying Jackie and I split up because it's fashionable?

Michael   She lives in Islington, doesn't she?

Matt   Nothing to do with me telling her I'm gay?

Michael   Yeah that's trendy too. I mean whoever wants to be a straight, white, heterosexual, married couple nowadays? Anyway, it was mutually agreed, the flat came with the café, they had nothing else.

Gary   Pity your dad was in the flat though, eh?

Michael She didn't know anything about that – still doesn't.

Gary You say.

Michael I say.

Gary My mum knew. She always said she didn't but she did, just turned a blind eye.

Michael We have led different lives, Gary, strange as it may seem, we're not twins, you know.

Gary I know, I know. Good thing too, be awful if we were twins and you were still brain dead, wouldn't it?

Michael You saying my mum knows?

Gary Why don't you ask her?

Michael Why don't you go fuck yourself, Gary?

Gary OK, if I go fuck myself then will you ask her?

Michael *talking to audience.*

Michael God, I've had enough. Everybody's got an opinion. No facts. Just opinions. Like they know me better than I know myself. I could get along just fine if . . . if everybody else was different, if everybody else just shut the fuck up and let me get on with it. (*Pause. Then sings.*) 'Come in, she says, I'll give you shelter from the storm . . .' I don't think my mum knows anything, I think she's too busy being 'artistic' with Clive. Anyway so what? What's the point of asking her? I'd rather not know, I know already, she knows nothing. (*Pause.*) Trouble with me is I'm the eternal optimist – unlike Gary, Gary is such a pessimist. When someone jumps on Gary he says 'Yeah so? My own fault, must be more careful next time.' But if someone did something nice for Gary, I swear he'd sue them for breach of contract, stab them for causing grievous emotional harm. And Matt's just as bad, trying to make out I've got some kind of problem. Never happy with me just being me. I do love Becky though, she's so cute. Me, I believe in happy endings, believe everything will sort itself out, eventually.

Trouble is I want it sorted yesterday. (*Sings.*) 'Come in, she says, I'll give you shelter from the storm.' (*To* **Matt**.) If I go and see my mum when it's raining she opens the door and sings that at me. Every time. 'Come in, she says, I'll give you shelter from the storm.' Every time. Pathetic. Sometimes I'll go just because it's raining, just to hear her say it, then I can say 'pathetic' and leave again. It's the little things that give me pleasure.

Ed   You're making that up.

Michael   What?

Ed   You don't really say 'pathetic' and then leave again. You say 'Hello, Mum, had any books published yet?' Then you'll stay just long enough to get into an argument, or if Clive's around you'll get into an argument immediately. Has she had one published yet?

Michael   No.

Ed   Hum ... Quick drink?

Michael   Yeah why not.

Ed   And I mean quick, told you before if you're going to visit, visit earlier, too old for these midnight rambles – and your friend's no spring chicken, whatever his name is.

Michael   This is Matt; Matt, this is Ed, my dad.

Matt   Oh so this is (*Looking around.*) ... oh er hi, Ed.

Ed   'Oh so this is' what?

Matt   Erm a nice place.

Michael *highly amused by* **Ed**.

Ed   You mean this is 'that stupid hippy bar with the mountain of junk stuck on the walls and games of chess played in poky corners by pseudo intellectuals, who usually turn out to be teachers, all of whom actually believe they are the actual generation that Bob Dylan actually spoke for and all call themselves left-wing liberals but Michael calls idiots'?

Matt   Erm . . .

Ed   Don't worry it's a well rehearsed paragraph he trots out to all his friends. Designed to wind me up but actually I think it's a pretty accurate description. Michael rehearses everything, don't you? He's also a great embellisher and an inveterate story-teller, but only out of idle amusement. I suppose he has to think about something while he's . . . You in the same line of business, Matt?

Matt   No I work for the council.

Ed   Um thought not.

Michael   Not sexy enough.

Ed   Don't want to tread on anybody's toes. So what's the connection a sort of boyfriend type thing?

Matt   Yeah.

Ed   Yeah what? A boyfriend or a type thing?

Michael *laughs.*

Matt   Boyfriend.

Ed   Thought so.

Ruth *potters in, clearing up. She startles* **Michael**, *he watches her, bemused, taking note,* **Ed** *noting* **Michael***'s reaction.*

Ed   Yeah so, if Dylan's mentioned in any way he instantly finds fault with everybody, it's his way of rebelling againt his parents – he would have done drugs but we did them first.

Matt   Well, you did a good job because Michael just hates any sort of drugs, won't have anything to do with them, won't even . . .

Matt *notices the focus has shifted to* **Ruth** *pottering. Then* **Ruth** *realises she's being watched.*

Ruth (*smiling*)   Some problem?

Ed (*puts his arm round her shoulder*)   Ruth, this is Michael and his friend Matt.

Ruth   The famous wayward Michael?

Ed   The very one.

Ruth   Well hello, I've been hearing all about you, in fact I believe I'm sleeping in your old bed.

Michael   Oh?

Ed   Had the sheets changed though, finally.

Ruth   I should think so too. Mind you, that's all down to me, men may be able to cook, but unless they're gay they can't . . . clean – oops.

Matt *and* **Ed** *chuckle,* **Michael** *still bemused.*

Ed   Something wrong, Michael?

Michael   No, no. Just erm a bit surprised, that's all.

Ed   I'm sorry I should have said. Ruth's my new assistant, well new, she's been here a while now.

Michael   She's living here.

Ruth   Er . . . yeah.

Ed (*puts an arm round* **Michael***'s neck*)   It's OK, don't worry, if ever you're stuck there's always the spare bedroom.

Ruth   Provided we . . .

Ed   Provided we've got clean sheets that is. (*Chuckle.*) I've always said if things don't work out there's always a place for you here, and I still mean it, nothing's changed. OK?

Michael   Yeah, yeah, it's . . . fine.

Ed   Good. Now, another drink. Matt? Michael?

Matt   Please.

Michael (*still slightly bemused*)   Yeah why not.

Awkward silence while **Ed** *gets the drinks sorted.*

Ruth   So, Matt, you an outreach worker for the homeless too?

Michael *talking to audience.*

Michael   Something funny going on. Something not right. He's never had live-in help before, never wanted to have anybody, there, in the flat. It's his kingdom, his place. The café's his public arena and the flat's his private one.

Matt   Well, it's probably just like he said, he needs an assistant.

Michael   No.

Matt   Well, you can't run a place like that single-handed.

Michael   He's always had temporary help, part-timers.

Matt   Well, perhaps he just wants a change.

Michael   No.

Matt   What's the problem, Michael? So what? Are you worried he might be involved with her or something? Well like, you know, he's a grown man, an adult, he has needs too.

Michael   She said she's sleeping in my room.

Matt   Well then? What's the problem?

Michael   Something's going on.

Gary   Yeah must be. I wouldn't trust that fucker further than I could throw him.

Michael   You don't understand, Gary.

Gary   Oh try me, Michael, go on try me. What's the difference between us huh? Not a lot I'll bet.

Michael   You know what your dad did, I don't.

Gary   Yeah so? Are you saying you can't remember some things? That happens to all of us, it's called blocking it out, that's normal.

Michael   No, I don't mean that.

Gary   What then? Do you think you liked it? Some of it? Do you think you might have initiated it sometimes?

Michael (*to* **Matt**)   So you liked him then?

Matt   Yeah I think he's a great guy.

Michael   You didn't think he was a bit . . . funny?

Matt   I thought he was very funny, similar sense of humour to yours, never know whether the two of you are joking or what?

Michael   No I meant funny odd?

Matt   Funny odd? I thought you were a bit funny odd.

Michael   Where did she come from?

Matt   What?

Michael   Well, where was she? She wasn't there when we arrived. She'd been upstairs. Why had she been upstairs? When they're closing up, when everything needs doing downstairs. No point in going upstairs? When you're closing up? What would she be checking for? What was she doing?

Matt   Are you jealous, Michael?

Michael   Jealous?

Matt   Of someone sleeping in your old room?

Michael   No of course not, I left years ago.

Gary   Did you talk to her at all? Find out how she got the job or why she got the job?

Michael   No, didn't stay that long.

Matt   Is it because she's not your mum?

Michael   What?

Gary   How old is she? About?

Michael   What?

Matt Do you feel sort of upset that your dad's got another woman?

Gary Is she your age?

Matt Do you want to talk about it, Michael?

Michael No.

Gary Is that what's wrong? Your dad's living with someone your own age?

Michael No.

Michael *talking to audience.*

Michael I love my dad. I love my dad so much. For years, since I was six it was me and him, him and me. We were like that, we were so close. There were times I could've killed him, there were. Times I hated him, hated what he did, but he never hurt me, never did anything really bad. Except of course when he stopped. When it all stopped, just sort of sudden. But it wasn't sudden really, when I think back, I suppose it got less and less, but it seemed sudden to me. That very last time and then waiting, months and months of waiting and nothing happened. He never came, never said anything, it was just like it never happened in the first place. I felt worse then, that was the worst time, I thought I'd done something, thought he was mad at me or didn't love me any more or something I just . . . (*Shouts.*) WHY DID IT STOP? God, you drove me mad. Nothing ever being said, everything covered up, normal, up in the morning, off to school, bright, breezy, sitting on the bus thinking, not sure, not wanting to be sure, did you think about it? Did you ever think about it the next day? You never said anything! It was always so silent, wasn't it? So unacknowledged. I don't even remember how it started. Too young. That's the point of it, isn't it, get the kid young and he won't understand. That drift, that slow, steady, knowing drift, so clever, so steady, all the time in the world, little by little, bit by bit, so the kid won't know, so that everything becomes blurred and . . . sliding. It just slid, it just slid to a point where I couldn't say stop, I couldn't say . . . anything because . . . because . . . exactly that. The slide down.

Matt Your dad's OK, isn't he? Pretty good I reckon. Me, I have to foist my boyfriends onto my parents. They never ask. Like when you were supposed to go with me? They knew you were coming, but when I got there they didn't say anything, didn't ask where you were or what had happened. They tolerate it all but they don't want to know, and certainly aren't going to ask.

Michael What's going on, Gary? Something's going on.

Gary Like what?

Michael I don't know but there's something making me panic and I don't know why, something making me feel like shit and I don't know why. But I keep thinking I should do, I know I should do.

Gary Well, what's changed?

Michael She's there. She's in my place. He had no right to let her, upstairs is my kingdom, downstairs is his. That's how it always was. Upstairs belongs to me, I ran it, I controlled it and he has no right to let anybody up there, without my say so, without consulting me.

Gary Your dad fucked you, didn't he, Michael?

Michael Yes, fucking yes, fucking yes, yes, yes.

Gary OK. Now we're getting somewhere.

Video diary.

Michael *talking live with simultaneous video projection.*

Michael I don't know what the problem is. I don't know why it's bothering me so much. It's just . . . with her there, suddenly everything seems so false and . . . sordid. I have an image . . . a memory of me and my dad in the flat, it's like a bubble, a dream. And it was all so . . . innocent and loving and . . . I don't think that's true any more. I'm beginning to think I invented that image . . .

Michael *is interrupted by* **Gary**.

Gary You've turned your phone off.

Michael I know.

Gary *waggles the phone at the camera.*

Gary That's not going to pay the rent, is it?

Onstage.

Matt *sitting, reading a newspaper.* **Michael** *just sitting, still for a while but then restless.*

Matt I told you to sit still.

Michael *tries to sit still again, but gets fidgety.*

Matt What's the problem?

Michael I want to do something.

Matt We are doing something.

Michael No, I mean something else. I'm just not into it today.

Matt Well I am.

Michael *sits still again, but gets restless.* **Matt** *finally puts newspaper down and goes over to* **Michael**, *puts his arms around his neck.*

Matt You're restless.

Michael Yeah.

Matt Can't wait today.

Michael *finding it difficult as* **Matt** *gets sexual.* **Michael** *succumbing (reluctantly) till* **Ed** *takes over from* **Matt**, *then* **Michael** *freaks.*

Michael Stop it! Stop it! I can't stand it!

Ed *backs off,* **Matt** *takes over.*

Matt What's the problem? What's wrong?

Michael Just ... don't.

Matt I thought you were into it?

Michael I wasn't. I said.

Matt I thought that was a joke – part of it.

Michael Well it wasn't.

Pause.

Matt What's wrong, Michael?

Michael You don't listen to me that's what. When I say I don't want it, I mean I don't want it.

Matt So what about the time when you say you don't want it and you do?

Michael OK, OK, don't start.

Matt No not OK. Because I don't know what's wrong with you lately but I'm really getting fed up with not knowing what you want.

Michael So? What do you want to do about it then?

Matt I want you to tell me what's bothering you?

Michael You are, that's what. You're bothering me.

Matt OK fine. So maybe we should cool it for a while.

Michael If that's what you want.

Matt No not what I want, what you want.

Michael Oh yeah go on, lay it all on me.

Matt You're the one that started it.

Michael Oh why? Because I won't fuck on demand? Because I won't drop my pants every time you click your fingers?

Matt Oh that is unfair. That is really unfair. What about the times when you don't want me to say anything at all and just strip you and fuck you? What about the times

when I've asked you and you've gotten irritated because
I've asked you? What about the times when you've gotten
irritated because for once I'd like you to take the initiative?
What about all the times I've gotten irritated because you
expect me to make all the running? Don't tell me I expect
you to fuck on demand, because you like it that way!

Michael Oh go fuck yourself, Matt.

Matt No, you go fuck yourself, Michael!

Gary Straight gays, they haven't a clue.

Michael Leave me alone, Gary, I just want to be alone.

Video.

External. Park. **Michael**, **Matt** *and* **Becky** *playing happily.*
Matt *and* **Michael** *taking it in turns to 'hold the camera'.*
Various cuts: **Michael** *pushing* **Becky** *on the swings.* **Matt** *and*
Becky *on the seesaw.* **Michael** *catching* **Becky** *jumping off a*
wall, holding her to him, both cheek to cheek, smiling into the camera.
Then a long shot of **Matt** *playing football with* **Becky**, **Michael**
simultaneously recording his voice-over.

Michael *(V.O.)* God, I love this, this is my family. How
can anyone want to ruin a little kid like Becky? How can
they even think of it? What did my dad think? What did
he see? Innocence. And she smells . . . nice, clean. No dirty
sweaty smell of sex. And little white socks, she's got lovely
legs, her skin all smooth and new and . . . a little dress that
shows her knickers and a tiny, perfect little bum
underneath. And she wouldn't know, wouldn't understand if
a finger strayed where it shouldn't. And that would be the
start. Start with one little . . . touch, almost accidental.
Nothing happens, because she doesn't know what that
touch means. And then having touched once, the next one
will be easier and more . . . sexual. And because she didn't
complain about the first touch she can't complain about the
next one. And on and on till she's overpowered by her
confusion and her guilt. Oh God . . . Oh God, Dad, I
loved you so much.

Video clicks off, (interrupted by **Gary***).*

Onstage.

Gary   What you watching?

Michael   Nothing.

Gary   Let's have a look.

Michael   No, it's private.

Gary   I thought you were making a video diary for the telly?

Michael   I am.

Gary   Well, how can it be private then?

Michael   It's private till it's edited.

Silence.

Gary   You still bothered about that Matt guy?

Michael   No.

Gary   Still bothered about your dad?

Michael   No.

Silence.

Gary   How come I never met him?

Michael   What do you want to meet him for, you've always said you hated him?

Gary   Not your dad, Matt.

Michael   You've always hated him too.

Gary   Only because I knew it wouldn't last.

Michael   Well, there you are, you were right, weren't you, happy now?

Pause.

Gary   Two friends in the whole world. That's all you've got, Michael, just two friends. Me and yourself.

Michael So?

Gary So why didn't you introduce me to Matt?

Michael What for?

Gary You introduced him to your dad.

Michael That was different.

Gary How?

Michael Just was.

Gary Are there similarities?

Michael Huh?

Gary Between Matt and your dad?

Michael Fuck off, Gary.

Gary Why didn't you introduce me then?

Michael I don't know.

Gary Why not? One good reason why not?

Michael Because I can't trust you to keep your fucking mouth shut, that's why not.

Gary About what?

Michael You know about what.

Gary About renting?

Michael He knows about that.

Gary So it's just about your dad then right? So why did you take Matt to meet him in the first place?

Silence.

Because you wanted to start the conversation, a way of letting him know, surely? Or maybe hoping he might guess, make it easier? Surely it was because you wanted him to see what a sexual abuser looks like? Right? Show him what you had to put up with? Who taught you your skills? Yeah?

Silence.

Or was it the other way round? You were just showing Ed that you've got a new dad now, one who still likes to fuck you? Saying 'Look, Dad, here's another shithead who can stick his dick in my arse any time he damn well pleases'? Maybe Matt just wanted to go round and thank the guy who'd made your arse so easy access in the first place? – just wanted to thank him for his years of endeavour? His sacrifice on the behalf of others? Perhaps they wanted to exchange notes on your performance and abilities? Maybe get together and have a little party – oh no, I forgot you're too old for your dad now, aren't you? Eh, Michael? Michael?

Michael I can't do it, Gary, not like you. I want somebody, need somebody like . . . That's not true, is it? Matt's not a bit like . . .

Both **Matt** *and* **Ed** *wave and smile at* **Michael** *in the same way.*

Gary Oh God, you've got to get your head sorted out. I seriously think it's about time you got yourself straight. Michael, are you listening? Dump your dad, forget him, he's a shithead. Be honest. Tell this Matt guy, if you want to, if you're serious about him. Tell him, tell me and tell yourself what an absolute bastard your dad is and then forget him – or else go over – one last time! – and beat the crap out of him, I'll help, tell Matt and he can help too. All three of us, beat the shit out of him, once and for all, and then enough huh? What do you think? . . .

Michael Gary? Would you like to meet Matt sometime?

Gary Tell you the truth, Michael, I'm not bothered either way, but if it would make you happy, why not?

Both laugh.

Michael (*to himself/audience*) Because it wouldn't make me happy, that's why not.

Video.

Gary *talking live with simultaneous video projection.*

Gary   I'm doing this because my friend Michael has asked me to. He wants to be on telly, have fifteen minutes of fame. I think he's an arsehole, but, because he's my friend I'm doing it. See, really, I couldn't give a toss what people think. I have nothing in common with other people. As far as I'm concerned other people are hypocrites or punters – or both. There's always an ulterior motive. Nobody does something for nothing. It's a hobby with me now, trying to work out what someone wants. I'm getting quite good at it too, spotting the subtext. It's all power in one form or another. One person trying to get power over another, trying to look big by stepping on someone. Me and my friends we manipulate for money, it's black and white, most people hate us for that. They hate us because our ulterior motive is so clear, so blatant. They hate us because we're honest, because we're not scurrying around trying to hide our manipulation, trying to cover up our power games. We're not tarting up our greed and selfishness with pathetic words like love or friendship. My friends are the only people I trust. My friends are honest. Of my friends there is only one who wasn't abused as a child, and I think he's a liar. So as far as I'm concerned everybody else can go fuck themselves.

Onstage.

Michael   I suppose you want an apology?

Matt   An explanation would be better.

Gary   Tell him, Michael, why not?

Michael   My dad bothered me.

Matt   What do you mean?

Gary   If he really cared about you what difference would it make?

Michael (*to* **Gary**)   Don't you feel in the least bit . . . a little bit . . . guilty?

Gary About what?

Michael I don't know . . . about your mum and dad?

Gary Why should I?

Michael (*to* **Matt**)   I want to be like Gary.

Matt Who's Gary?

Michael Gary's a friend, known him for years, and Gary can do it, Matt. He can do anything – alone. He's got nobody.

Matt Perhaps he's got you.

Michael No, my dad's all I've got. See my mum, she . . . well she's got Clive, she doesn't want me, she pretends to, she says she does, well she doesn't, she's never even said that, all she ever said was I was settled. Settled with my dad. Which I . . . was.

Matt But not any more?

Michael *looks momentarily worried.*

Michael It's just about this Ruth woman, that's all.

Matt Michael, why don't you talk to your mum about it?

Michael I do talk to her.

Matt Get things sorted out.

Michael They are.

Matt Are they? Really?

Michael We have talked, it's OK, no worries.

Matt Well, you could always talk to me, you know, I'm not averse to a bit of agony aunting.

Gary Unless of course you feel ashamed about telling him. If so you're an arsehole because there's nothing for you to feel ashamed about. Let your dad feel ashamed, he's the real fucker.

Michael   Gary? Do you totally hate your mum and dad?

Gary   Too right I do.

Michael   Really? I mean really, honestly?

Gary (*hesitant*)   No, not totally.

Michael *touches* **Gary**'s *shoulder in sympathy – holds it there.*

Michael   Matt, I . . . I don't want to be like Gary.

Matt *puts his arm round* **Michael**, **Michael** *still touching* **Gary**'s *shoulder.*

Matt   You won't be, you've got me.

Matt *and* **Michael** *snog.* **Michael**'s *hand sliding from* **Gary**'s *shoulder to his wrist, so that whilst snogging, he's still holding onto* **Gary**.

Video.

External. **Michael**, *dressed sexily, young, sitting on the safety railing on the 'meat rack'.*

Gary (*V.O. – concerned*)   What are you doing this for Michael? This is ridiculous.

A car horn sounds. **Michael** *jumps off rail and, after a cursory chat gets into the car.*

Gary (*V.O.*)   Arsehole.

Onstage.

A battered and bruised looking **Michael**.

Matt   Jesus Christ, what happened to you?

Michael   Three of them, two hiding behind the seats, next thing I know it's a tie round the neck and all hell breaks loose.

Matt   Oh God, Michael, you've got to quit, it's ridiculous, you can't live like this.

Michael   And do what? I can't do anything else.

Gary You're just going to have to bounce back.

Michael For what? To get punched again?

Gary No not to get punched again. Because let's face it, it was your own fault.

Michael Oh thanks, Gary.

Matt Move in, live with me for a while till you get organised, there's loads of things you could do if you put your mind to it.

Michael And what about when Becky comes? You said yourself we have to be careful about Jackie.

Matt We'll sort something out.

Gary You should've checked the car, everybody knows you should check the car!

Michael I did check the car they were hiding behind the seats.

Gary Well then what were you checking for if not to check if anybody was hiding behind the seats? No point in checking to see if he's got a stereo and a heater, check to see if there's gonna be sounds and warmth while you're being beaten to a raw and bloody pulp. No this is a good thing. Get you out of your stew. It's nice to hear some good news for a change.

Michael Oh ha ha.

Matt Besides it was only about the prostitution. If you're not a prostitute then Jackie's not going to mind, right?

Michael Oh ha ha.

Gary No seriously. Because next time you're thinking about slumming it, you're going to check that car real well, with a fine tooth comb. And let's face it, you could have been murdered.

Michael Thanks, Gary, that's cheered me up no end.

Matt No I'm serious. She knows about you, obviously, so you moving in, well, it must have crossed her mind that you might. And OK so she resents you a bit, is a bit unhappy about you being around Becky . . .

Michael Thanks, Matt, that's cheered me up no end.

Matt No, we just have to prove to her that you're OK, that you can be trusted, and if you're not doing this stuff any more, if you're a regular bloke with a regular job . . .

Michael Regular blokes aren't into kids I suppose.

Matt I don't mean that, she doesn't mean that.

Michael What do you and she mean then?

Matt 'Prostitute' isn't the best role model you could present to a child of Becky's age.

Michael What's the matter, you think I might sit down and discuss the ins and outs of cock sucking with her?

Matt No.

Michael What then?

Matt Just quit, Michael, please, it would be better for all of us.

Michael And do what, Matt? What would be acceptable?

Gary Pick yourself up, brush yourself down,

Michael Get punched all over again.

Gary Whatever. What's the alternative?

Ruth Well hello again! My God, what happened to you?

Michael Bit of a fight, nothing serious.

Ruth The homeless getting touchy huh?

Michael Something like that.

Ed *appears.*

Ed Well, my goodness, twice in a month, I'm honoured. Ugh no I'm not, I'm needed – what happened?

Slight awkward pause.

Ruth   Well, I must check on Jake, excuse me.

Ed   So what happened? Pick a wrong one? Luck run out? Or is this the latest fashion – look tough but woebegone? Whatever, I expect you need a drink.

Michael   Who's Jake?

Ed   Jake?

Michael   Yes Jake.

Ed   Ruth's son. Have you seen a doctor or does it look worse than it is?

Michael   I'm fine. You didn't tell me Ruth had a son?

Ed   Thought Ruth would have told you. No big deal.

Michael   How old is he?

Ed   It's no big deal, Michael.

Michael   How old?

Ed   Dunno. Seven or eight I suppose.

Michael *slams his drink down,* **Ed** *grabs his arm.*

Ed   It's not what you're thinking.

Michael   Isn't it?

Ed   No. Listen . . .

Michael   Isn't it?

Ed   Listen, Michael . . .

Michael   What is it then?

Ed *grabs* **Michael** *to him, hugs him tightly, almost restraining him.*

Ed   You and me, Michael, what happened, we should have talked about it, we should maybe talk about it now. Listen to me because I don't think you understand. And I want you to. I felt . . . terrible. It was a long time ago and

it didn't last. Remember? It didn't last long, it hardly
happened really, I was . . . when your mum left I was . . .
unhappy and . . . well it was like a bit of a crisis, I was
going through a bit of a crisis and I didn't mean it to
happen, things got out of hand, but it wasn't much, even
then, not much happened, did it, really? And God, you'll
never know how much I regretted it, how bad I felt. I went
too far I know I did, just a little bit too far with our
horseplay and joking around, it was accidental really, I
hadn't meant for it to happen, I wasn't even too sure if
you noticed that it had happened. That's why I never said
anything. Didn't want to confuse you, didn't want you to
think that it was more than it was, build it up in your
mind. I was good to you though, wasn't I, Michael? After
your mum left? After she walked out on us? I tried my
best, I knew she'd upset you, I tried so hard to give you
the love that you needed, tried so hard to fill that gap that
she'd made. If I perhaps loved you too much, if I perhaps
compensated too much when your mum went. I felt so bad
you see? So bad that she went without you, wanted to
make it up to you. But it wasn't much, I didn't do much,
did I? Nothing bad really. Hardly anything if you
remember correctly. We should have talked about it sooner
I know and if I confused you all those years ago then I'm
sorry, I didn't mean to, I just didn't want to blow it out of
proportion – such a little thing, a slight . . . mistake. Eh,
Michael? A slight mistake that happened once, that I've
never done before or since. The sort of thing that's perhaps
best . . . forgotten, eh? What do you think?

Michael I think you're pressing on my bruises.

Ed *lets go.*

Michael Got my ribs kicked.

Ed I'm sorry.

Silence.

Michael Why is she here?

Ed I needed an assistant, she needed accommodation,

she's cheap.

Michael And Jake?

Ed That's why she needed accommodation. It's what your mum should have done, with you.

Silence.

Michael You abused me.

Ed If you think that I'm sorry.

Michael And Jake?

Ed No, Michael, believe me, nothing like that.

Michael I need somewhere to stay for a while. Here. I need to stay here for a while. Fix it for me will you.

Michael *talking to audience.*

Michael Lies all lies. Sometimes I wonder though, sometimes I think it's me. I mean I do lie, on occasion, but I've always thought I knew when, maybe I don't. Maybe I've told myself a lie for so long that I've forgotten it wasn't true. I'm not even sure it actually happened. Or what actually happened.

Video.

Internal. In the flat above **Ed***'s café/bar.* **Michael** *filming his old bedroom, voice-over.* **Ruth** *in the frame to begin with, caught unawares. She pushes the camera away, half friendly, half irritated, and leaves.*

Michael (*V.O.*) This is my old bedroom. It's changed a bit now, posters and stuff, all my old gear's gone, obviously. Wallpaper's the same though, furnishings, same old crap. Two beds in at the moment, one for Jake, not usually so cramped. This is the only room with curtains, everywhere else has blinds, those Chinese bamboo things, the sort you can see through. That's a massive hint or clue, isn't it, for anyone who wants to look for hints or clues. There used to be a Spiderman duvet cover on that bed. Weaving his web of deceit under my Spiderman duvet ha ha. Don't know what happened to it.

He continues filming, panning throughout the flat.

Michael (*V.O.*) God this place is a tatty old mess. Boxes and rubbish and sixties hippy crap. Nothing's changed, just seems worse than I remember it. Like living in a storeroom.

Onstage.

Michael Don't you ever find the flat gets on your nerves?

Ruth How do you mean?

Michael Well, all the boxes and stock and piles of junk? I mean, it's really disorganised, don't you find? With Jake and everything?

Ruth Jake?

Michael Yeah. Well, I dunno I mean, I don't know what it does to Jake, I was just remembering how it used to drive me crazy, you know when I was his age sort of thing.

Ruth Really? It used to bother you?

Michael Like mad.

Ruth I didn't think boys bothered about that sort of thing.

Michael Oh you'd be surprised.

Ruth What're you getting at, Michael?

Michael Nothing. (*Friendly, jokey.*) Oh let's face it it's a pigsty up there, my dad's a slob, always has been. Well up there anyway, down here, well it's all fur coat and no knickers, isn't it?

Ruth (*laughs in agreement*) Well, maybe.

Michael Still nothing to do with me, for all I know you might want Jake to grow up a cleanliness obsessed, anally retentive, feather dustered old queen, and why not, some of my best friends have Hoover attachments.

Ruth *laughs quizzically.*

Michael   You know what? I like this.

Ruth   What?

Michael   This place, having you and Jake around, it's nice. Hated it before, when I was here alone, dad working and everything but it's nice now.

Ruth   Uh huh?

Michael   What?

Ruth   Does this mean you're moving back permanently?

Michael (*laughs*)   No. Don't worry I'll be gone soon, I know when I'm not wanted. Jake can have his room back, you can get some peace – and space.

Ruth   Wonderful.

Michael   Mind you, you know, if you and Jake are cramped in that one room, well, Jake could always move back into my room.

Ruth *gives him a look.*

Michael   I wouldn't mind squeezing in with you, we could always huddle together for warmth.

Ruth   It's not cold and you're gay.

Michael   Who said that?

Ruth   Your dad.

Michael   He doesn't know everything.

Ruth   And you just said you were a feather dustered old queen.

Michael   I said some of my friends were – nothing old about me.

Ruth And then there's the little matter of your boyfriend, Matt?

Michael Doesn't mean I can't swing both ways – if the need arises.

Ruth If the what arises?

Michael The need, Need. I don't mind sacrificing myself on the altar of heterosexuality for the good of you and Jake's comfort. I could quite easily go for you.

Ruth Oh really, I'm touched.

Michael Who by? Ed?

Ruth What?

Michael Have you been touched by Ed?

Ruth Oh, Michael.

Michael Well, it's possible, you're very good-looking, and you seem very friendly with each other.

Ruth Yes just friendly.

Michael Has he ever tried it on or anything?

Ruth No.

Michael What not even a little bit?

Ruth No.

Michael What about Jake. (*Laughs.*)

Ruth What?

Michael Well why not? He sticks it in the trifle.

Ruth (*laughing*) That's disgusting. You've got a warped mind.

Michael And why do you think his quiches are so tasty? Have you ever seen him actually making one?

Ed *enters, stands watching them laugh.*

Ed What's the joke?

Michael Just talking about sex. How you do it, why you do it, who you do it with.

Ed Haven't you got something better to do?

Ruth *obliges to move and look busy.*

Michael Er no, I haven't actually.

Ed *leaves irritated.*

Ruth You two aren't getting on too well, are you?

Michael We're getting on like a house on fire.

Ruth Oh well, I'll expect blazing rows any day now.

Michael *chuckles.*

Michael Ah we get on really. Actually it's like I said, the flat upstairs, the mess. I think it makes everybody tetchy. Don't you?

Ruth Well, I suppose it is a bit of a mess but . . .

Michael Do you want me to ask him for you? If we could tidy it up a bit?

Ruth No, not with the tension you're creating. I'll ask him.

Michael OK.

He smiles.

Video diary.

Michael *talking live with simultaneous video projection.*

Michael If he is doing stuff with Jake then I'm just a body. Nothing special. Easy access, cheap, rent boy. Ten a penny on the meat rack. Didn't want me. Wanted what he could get from me. It never occurred to me that there might be . . . might have been . . . others. I would've known, never said I was coming, never . . . I wasn't just a body, it was never like that. He's not a punter he's my dad and what he says about Jake I believe him. Because I came

lots of times, unannounced, checking, keeping my eye on
him, been keeping my bloody, fucking eye on him for
years. And never, not once, there was only me, there only
ever was me. Because if there had been, if I'd found out
there had been others ... I was the one he wanted, not a
body, not a rent boy, prostitute, cheap, shitty little easy
shag. Wasn't just because I was there, available for him
because she went ... He had it perfect, the set up couldn't
have been more perfect, whenever he wanted it, however
he wanted it, nobody to stop him, no questions asked,
nobody to notice, and me, he knew I wouldn't say anything
because oh ... because I hate her, because I wanted her so
much, because I knew she couldn't take me, knew she
couldn't help because ... because he said so. He's not
doing stuff with Jake. I know he's not. And I'm going to
make damn sure he's not. I'm not going to let him.

Onstage.

Bob Dylan music playing. **Ed** *closing up the bar,* **Michael** *sitting,
flicking absently through a paper. Tension between them, opposite ends
of the bar, long silence. Argument brewing.*

Ed   Aren't you bored?

Michael   Not yet.

Silence.

Ed   Haven't you got a job to go to?

Michael   Recuperating.

Silence.

Ed   Still looking for lies, are you?

Michael   No, too busy looking for truth.

Michael *flashes a very insincere smile.* **Ed** *irritated.* **Ruth** *enters.*

Ed (*quickly*)   East Finchley.

Michael *slight glance to register* **Ruth**'s *presence.*

Michael   Holloway Road.

Ed Goodge Street.

Ruth Mornington Crescent!

Ed *and* **Michael** *momentarily amused at the bluff.*

Ruth God, my feet are killing me. Why do some people have to be so bloody awkward? (*Sits.*)

Silence. **Ruth** *looks from one to the other, then at her watch.*

Ruth God, it's late. We were busy tonight.

Ed Yep. Some help would've been nice.

Ed *and* **Ruth** *look at* **Michael** *pointedly,* **Michael** *looks back unperturbed.*

Ruth I better check that Jake's still OK, still loads to clear up.

Ruth *gets up to move,* **Michael** *gets up.*

Michael I'll go.

Ruth It's OK I can . . .

Michael I can go – least I can do.

Ruth *sits down again, puts her feet up.* **Ed** *watches* **Michael** *leave, highly suspicious.*

Ruth Well, that was nice of him, I hate those stairs.

Ed *still watching the door, thoughtful, suspicious.*

Ruth Your Michael's OK, isn't he? When he's not being awkward.

Ed Yeah, Ruth, you know, if I were you I wouldn't trust Michael completely. In fact I wouldn't trust him as far as you could throw him.

Ruth *looks quizzical. Then* **Ed** *smiles, almost laughs, as though a joke. Then moves towards her.*

Ed Now, about your aching feet . . .

Ed *kneels to massage* **Ruth**'s *feet.* **Ruth** *still half quizzical.*

Video.

Internal. **Michael***'s old bedroom.* **Michael** *filming a sleeping* **Jake***, music quietly coming from downstairs.* **Michael** *enters, pans the gloomy room, the bed, up and down* **Jake***'s duvet-covered body. A quiet voice-over:*

Michael (*V.O.*)   It was always late. I pretended to be asleep. I was always awake but I pretended to be asleep. I think he liked it like that. I feel a bit like I used to, doing this, sort of . . . panicky I suppose. He'd creep. I could always hear him though, hear him rustling in the dark. Knew that any second now I'd feel that hand on my body. I could probably touch Jake, he's definitely asleep. I know how to, just slowly slip my hand under the duvet, quietly, silently. He'll just lie there, allow it to happen, be unable to . . .

Jake *stirs in his sleep. Video clicks off.*

Onstage.

Good-natured 'argument' as **Michael** *enters and stands, watching.*

Ed   What do you mean 'crap'?

Ruth   Sorry, I just can't bear him.

Ed   But his work's seminal, the guy's a genius.

Ruth   He can't sing, he's a smug wanker and he's crap.

Michael   Oh, Dylan . . .

Ed   Right! Right!

Ed *gets up to go to bar.*

Michael   Jake's fine. Dead to the world.

Ruth   Good. Thanks.

Ed *pauses to exchange looks with* **Michael***. Both suspicious of each other.*

Ed   For one thing he changed the course of musical history . . .

Behind bar a stack of Dylan albums that **Ed** *thumps on to bar counter.*

And, I know it's a cliché, but he did, he DID put poetry into the charts.

He rifles through albums.

Michael (*quiet*)   I'm going to bed.

Ed *triumphantly holding up record for* **Ruth** *to see as* **Michael** *departs.*

Ed   'Blood on the Tracks' . . .

Video.

Internal. **Ed**'s *flat.* **Ruth** *and* **Jake** *shifting and clearing junk.*

Onstage.

Michael *with his back to* **Ruth** *and* **Ed**, *smirking.* **Ed** *keeps moving, busy, trying to 'avoid' the argument.* **Ruth** *following him around, persistent.*

Ruth   I don't see what the problem is, I really don't. I mean why are you getting at me all of a sudden? I asked you and you said it was fine, you even admitted that the mess had gotten out of hand, you said it was a good idea.

Ed   Will you keep your voice down, I don't want the customers to hear.

Ruth   We haven't got any customers.

Ed   Well, there could be any minute. (*Stops.*) Look all I said was I can't find the bloody invoices. OK? That's all.

He busies himself again.

Ruth   Yes and over breakfast it was 'Where's my damn order book?', and while I'm trying to get Jake off to school it's 'I can't find a bloody thing in this place', and just when I think things are quiet I hear you booming 'Call this organised? Call this sorted?', just because you happened to stub your toe on the banister, which I haven't moved, obviously, or maybe it was because you could finally find the banister after all this time, I mean, did you even know you had one? Behind all that junk?

Ed Look, Ruth, I've got things to do, I don't have time to discuss this now.

Ruth So when have you got time? When exactly is the best time to find out why you've suddenly got a bee in your bonnet?

Michael (*to audience – smiling*) Ah memories, memories. Never any time to argue. Don't argue in front of the child, then don't argue in front of the customers. Keep it all bottled up. My dad hates arguments, wants everything to go his way.

Ruth God, what is it with you? You know Jake can't live in that mess, we agreed. I mean, fine for you down here all hours, but when Jake comes home he has to stay up there. And what if Jake decides to play with some stuff? Explore some of the boxes or something? Who's going to get blamed? Me. God, I'm trying to be reasonable, I know it's your place and everything, but you can't have it both ways.

Michael She shouldn't be doing that, it'll annoy him. Either be sweet to him, let him have his way – or bugger off.

Ed God, women. What is your problem? I can't find anything and you take it personally. Of course I can't find anything I don't know where you've put stuff! If you'd written a list. You could have written a list telling me what had gone where – but no you expect me to guess, like I've got time for that sort of caper.

Michael (*rubbing his hands gleefully*) · If it was good enough for my mum, it's good enough for Ruth. Well, even better in fact, quicker – she can take Jake with her.

Ruth I'm not being unreasonable, am I, Michael?

Michael I don't think so.

Ed Is that unreasonable, Michael, for her to just tell me what she's done, with my stuff?

Michael I don't think so.

Ed Is this your doing?

Michael What? Why should I be doing anything? You said yourself you're not into Jake or anything and I believe you. I'm just . . . recuperating.

Ed Don't push it, Michael. Don't push me.

Michael (*to himself/audience*) Why not? You pushed me for years.

Onstage. Night.

Ed *enters and connects* **Michael***'s video camera to his video projector in the bar. He watches* **Michael***'s video diary fast forward, playing occasional short snatches.*

Onstage.

Michael *'eavesdropping' on* **Ed** *and* **Ruth***.*

Ed (*sings*) 'I ain't looking to fight with you, frighten you or uptighten you. Drag you down or drain you down, chain you down or bring you down. All I really want to do is, baby, be friends with you.'

Ruth *gives him a curious look.*

Ed That's sort of my way of saying sorry.

Ruth Or Bob Dylan's way of saying sorry.

Ed It's as good as any.

Ruth Is it?

Ed Isn't it?

Ruth *smiles.*

Michael (*to himself/audience*) Shit.

Ed OK how about: I'm sorry I was booming around like a bear.

Ruth Sounds more honest.

Ed Less poetic.

Ruth More accurate.

Ed Less romantic.

Ruth What?

Michael (*to himself / audience*) What?

Ed *smiles, shrugs.*

Ed Just trying to be friendly.

Michael Flirting. He's trying to flirt with her.

Ruth So we're not getting under your feet then?

Ed What?

Ruth You're not fed up with us, with Jake and me?

Ed No, Christ, what makes you think that? I love having you here, both of you. I love it. And . . .

Ruth What?

Ed And . . . I love what you've done upstairs. I've never seen the place so tidy – or so organised. In fact, I'd go so far as to say it feels almost homelike, like a home.

Ed *smiles winningly.*

Michael He is flirting. He's flirting with her. I want them out! I want them to just leave!

Michael *approaches* **Ruth***, stands very close, almost face to face.*

Michael Ruth?

Ruth What?

Michael I'm really confused.

Ruth About what? . . . what?

Michael Do you fancy me?

Ruth (*friendly push*)   Oh, Michael.

Michael   Seriously.

Ruth   What?

Michael   Do you fancy me?

Ruth (*waiting for the punch line*)   Why?

Michael   Because ... because I don't know how to approach women.

Ruth   How do you mean?

Michael   I fancy a woman and I don't know how to approach her.

Ruth   Well, I should imagine you approach her the same way as you'd approach men.

Michael *grabs* **Ruth**'s *face and kisses her.*

Ruth   That's how you approach men?

Michael *looks worried.*

Ruth   No, Michael, this is the way you approach men.

Ruth *grabs* **Michael**'s *face and kisses him, both trying not to laugh.*

Michael   I've got a condom.

Ruth   Well, get on with it then.

They kiss again while fumbling to undo clothes etc. gradually falling below the bar counter. A while of that, then **Ed** *enters, carrying a bag, looks behind the bar.*

Ed   Oh my goodness, excuse me.

He walks away quickly into the customer area, his back to the bar, face raging, as **Michael** *and* **Ruth** *slowly peer their heads above the counter, then stand,* **Ruth** *embarrassed,* **Michael** *calculating. Before turning to face them,* **Ed**'s *face changes to a big grin.*

Ed   And I thought you were gay, Michael, tsk tsk. But hey! there's hope of a grandson after all. Hope you used a condom, God knows where Michael's been. Erm, one thing I should say though – if you must do that sort of thing, please don't do it behind the bar – well, not when we're open anyway, could put the customers off. Right, so, I've got to go out for a couple of hours so you two can get back to your shenanigans, ta ta!

Ruth *breathes a sigh of relief,* **Michael** *looks perturbed.*

Video.

Blank screen. Static.

Onstage.

Ruth, *worried, looking upwards to the flat as the noise of banging, crashing, door slamming and mayhem goes on above her. Then* **Michael** *entering, furious, destructively looking for something around the café, breaking glasses and sweeping things out of his way behind the bar.* **Ruth**, *terrified, uncomprehending.*

Ruth   Michael, what? What's the matter, what is it? What's wrong?

Michael *pacing the floor, still furious, wondering what to do.*

Michael   My tape, Gary, he's stolen my tape, the bastard's got my tape.

Gary   What?

Michael   Bloody done it to me again. That's private, like a diary and he's done it again, bloody fucked me again, I feel like he's fucked me again.

Gary   Who, Michael? Who has?

Michael   My dad, my dad's got my tape, my video, he's probably watched it, he'll know everything that's on it.

Gary   You've been to your dad's? All this time? What the hell for?

Michael   Because of Jake. I found out about Jake. There's nothing on it though, it's all about him. What's going on, Gary? Why was he smiling? All it says was how I loved him, all it said was the truth. What's he up to? It's got to be something to do with Ruth, has to be, because he wasn't bothered, he was smiling. So . . . Why?

Gary   What the hell are you going on about?

Michael   My dad's stolen my tape.

Gary   Yeah yeah I gathered that.

Michael   Fucking watched it and . . .

Gary   All right!

Michael (*a bit calmer*)   Personal stuff, Gary.

Gary   Yeah I get the picture. Your dad's stolen your video tape. And who are these other people?

Michael   What other people?

Gary   What was it? Ruth? and Jack? Luke?

Michael   Jake. See they're living there, at the flat and at first I tried to irritate them, but then when I saw him flirting with her I thought that was his plan so . . .

Gary   Who? This Ruth and Jake?

Michael   No, Ruth and my dad.

Gary   Right. So who's Jake?

Michael   Ruth's son. So then I . . .

Gary   What? How old?

Michael   Seven, eight. So I . . .

Gary   Oh fucking hell! So you told Ruth, told her to get the fuck out of there?

Michael   No. I . . .

Gary   Fucking hell, Michael, why not? Why the hell not?

Michael   I'm telling you! He was trying to flirt with her so I thought, right I'll put a stop to that . . .

Gary By telling her.

Michael No by fucking her. But it didn't work. He was smiling and then I found out he'd stolen my tape. So what's on the tape to make him think . . . ?

Gary Stuff your bloody tape, Michael. Why haven't you told her? Why?

Michael Because . . .

Gary Why?

Michael Because . . . Because I wanted them to leave for other reasons.

Gary What do you mean for other reasons?

Michael Oh shit!

Gary What?

Michael Shit, shit, shit, shit, shit. I made it better. Fuck me, Gary, I made it better. If I'm in with Ruth then Jake's on his own. He wasn't smiling about the tape, he was smiling about Jake. The tape's something else.

Gary *pushes* **Michael** *hard, down into a chair.*

Gary Forget about your tape! Forget about your fucking tape! A kid being abused and you're bothering about a tape? What is your problem? Now. Why haven't you told his mother? Why?

Michael Because . . .

Gary Why?

Michael Jake's not necessarily being . . .

Gary We're talking about your dad!

Michael Yeah and . . .

Gary So why haven't you told her?

Michael Because . . .

Gary Why?

Michael Because he's my dad.

Gary *hits him.*

Michael And because I love him.

Gary *hits him.*

Michael And he might love someone else.

Gary *hits him.*

Michael And I don't want him to stop loving me.

Gary *hugs him.*

Ed, **Ruth** and **Matt** *grouped together round the bar as though they have been talking earnestly. Silence as* **Michael** *enters and looks.*

Matt Michael! I've been looking all over for you!

Michael *shocked at* **Matt** *being there.*

Michael What are you doing here?

Matt I was looking for you, you didn't tell me where you were, I was worried.

Michael I've been here.

Matt Obviously.

Michael Well, now you know.

Matt Yes.

Michael Yes.

Michael *stares at* **Matt**, *expecting him to now go,* **Matt** *doesn't get the signal. Finally* **Michael** *turns to* **Ed**.

Where's my tape?

Ed *takes the tape out of his bag and holds it out to* **Michael**. **Michael** *snatches it from him.*

Michael You stole it.

Ed No I didn't. I found it in the video, I was going to give it to you but ... (*Glancing at* **Matt**.) I got distracted.

Michael   It wasn't in the video, I didn't leave it in the video.

Ed (*shrugs*)   Well, that's where I found it.

Michael *looks from* **Ed** *to* **Ruth**, *then back again*.

Michael   So how did it get there then?

Ed   No idea. Ruth?

Ruth   I don't touch other people's things.

Silence. **Michael** *having a slight doubt*.

Ed   Is that what all this mess was about? My bedroom looks like a demolition site.

Silence.

An apology would be nice.

Michael *pointedly turns to* **Ruth**.

Michael   I need to talk to you, privately.

Ed   Oh I don't think you should just abandon Matt, Michael . . .

Michael   I'm not abandoning him.

Ed (*ignoring* **Michael**'s *words*)   He's been worried sick about you, been running himself ragged trying to find you, the least you could do is stay, chat, have a drink, explain what you've been up to.

Michael *looks at* **Ed**.

Michael   I need to talk to Ruth.

Ed   I'm sure that can wait.

Matt   Look . . . er . . . If I'm in the way or something?

Ed   No you're fine, Matt. I can't think of anything that Michael would want to say to Ruth that we can't all hear. What do you think, Ruth?

Ruth *very embarrassed, shrugs her shoulders, looks to* **Michael** *for guidance. Awkward silence.*

Michael (*glancing between* **Ruth**, **Ed** *and* **Matt**)   Ruth? I . . . er . . . I'm sorry if I worried you at all when I was . . . rampaging.

Everybody visibly relaxes. Stand awkwardly in silence. **Gary** *enters.*

Gary   Sorry, Michael, mate, couldn't trust you.

Michael *spins towards* **Gary**, *surprised.* **Ed** *momentarily frowns.*

Gary   Have you told her? (*Looking at* **Ruth**.) Is this her?

Michael   Gary, leave it, please . . .

Ruth   Told me what?

Gary   Go on, do it.

Michael   Gary, just leave me alone . . .

Gary   OK I will. Ruth? You Ruth?

Ed (*calm*)   I think you should let Michael speak for himself. He can be incredibly eloquent when he wants to be, isn't that right, Michael? (*Pause.*) Like for instance when speaking to camera?

Michael   I knew you stole it, watched it.

Ed   Shall we let Ruth watch it? And what about Matt?

Gary *and* **Michael** *stare at* **Ed**, *surprised, then very suspicious.*

Matt   Is there something I should know about?

Ed   Michael?

Michael   Not here, not now.

Gary   Yes. Go on, Michael, call his bluff.

Michael   Matt, would you please leave?

Ed   Ah no, Michael, you should show Matt too.

Gary (*to* **Michael** *sotto voce*)   You didn't bloody tell Matt did you, arsehole!

Matt   Tell me what? What?

Gary   Go on, Michael, tell them.

Michael (*to* **Gary** *sotto voce*)   I can't.

Gary   Why not?

Michael   Because of Becky.

Gary   Who?

Matt   What's Becky got to do with anything?

Gary   Who the hell's Becky?

Pause. **Ed** *smiles, almost triumphant.*

Michael   Ruth, I've got to tell you about Jake . . .

Ed (*cutting through commandingly*)   OK, let's see it. Let's see the tape.

He puts his arm round **Ruth**, *ostensibly to move her in front of the video screen but also effectively pulling her away from* **Michael** *who is still holding the tape, bewildered.*

Don't worry, Michael, I made copies.

He places another tape in the VCR.

This is for you really, isn't it, Michael? Been trying to understand yourself, the way you are.

Michael *and* **Gary** *exchange looks.*

Ed   I only copied what seemed pertinent. Didn't think you'd want all the sordid details.

Michael *slowly realises what* **Ed***'s done to the tape. Everyone stands still, watching* **Ed***'s edited version.*

Video.

Cuts of **Michael** *speaking from previous scenes:*

Cut

'I get on well with my dad and I'd like to keep it that way, and if that means not talking about certain . . . events, then

so be it. I'd hate us to fall out over something as ...
meaningless as sex. Although I know some would regard
child sex as anything but meaningless but ... that's their
problem, I don't suffer from it.'

Cut

'Everyone's got an opinion. No facts. Just opinions. Like
they know me better than I know myself. I could get along
just fine if ... if everybody else was different, if everybody
else just shut the fuck up and let me get on with it.'

Cut

'Get the kid young and he won't understand. That drift,
that slow, steady, knowing drift, so clever, so steady, all the
time in the world, little by little, bit by bit, so the kid won't
know, so that everything becomes blurred and ... sliding.'

Cut

'I could probably touch Jake, he's definitely asleep. I know
how to, just slowly slip my hand under the duvet, quietly,
silently. He'll just lie there, allow it to happen, be unable
to ...' **Jake** *stirs in his sleep.*

Cut

'Innocence. And she smells ... nice, clean. No dirty sweaty
smell of sex. And little white socks, she's got lovely legs, her
skin all smooth and new and ... a little dress that shows
her knickers and a tiny, perfect little bum underneath. And
she wouldn't know, wouldn't understand if a finger strayed
where it shouldn't. And that would be the start. Start with
one little ... touch, almost accidental. Nothing happens,
because she doesn't know what that touch means. And then
having touched once, the next one will be easier and more
... sexual. And because she didn't complain about the first
touch she can't complain about the next one.'

Cut

'And I think Matt trusts me.'

Cut

'I suppose having Becky attracted me to him even more.'

Cut

Michael *catching* **Becky** *jumping off a wall, holding her to him, both cheek to cheek, smiling into the camera.*

Freeze-frame last shot a long time, then the video goes off, static.

Blackout.

All Over Lovely

All Over Lovely was first performed at the Traverse Theatre, Edinburgh, on 8 August 1996. The cast was as follows:

A   Claire Dowie
B   Peta Lily

Directed by Colin Watkeys

B You came.

A I was curious.

B Curiosity killed the cat.

A Better to be a cat than a bitch.

B What's that supposed to mean?

A Means you're a bitch of course.

B Why? What makes you say that?

A You know why.

B I don't, I've no idea. Have I upset you?

A Of course you upset me, you went to Australia, didn't you.

B Oh God, are you still harking on that? That was years ago.

A So? You hadn't seen your mother in years but you still went.

B That's totally different.

A How?

B She's my mother.

A So?

B So you're not.

A You're my sister, almost . . .

B Oh God.

A . . . my lover, almost.

B That was a phase we went through.

A Well I'm still going through it, OK?

B Oh, grow up, get over it.

A And do what?

B Learn to love somebody else.

A Well allow me to then, stop bothering me.

B I just thought you'd be interested, this is going to be a revolution.

A Well I like a good revolution, who's in charge?

B We all are.

A What does that mean?

B Means we all agree to go along with the consensus.

A Doesn't sound like much of a revolution to me.

B Be patient, the world's going to change.

A Are you sure?

B The patriarchal hierarchy will topple and be replaced by a fairer, more equitable society.

A Will every man, woman and child be given due respect and be allowed to fulfil their potential?

B Of course and women will end up on top.

A On top of what?

B On top of whoever's underneath.

A Will we be lovers?

B Yes we'll be lovers.

A And what about Australia?

B You mustn't upset yourself with thoughts of Australia.

A Will Australia be forgotten?

B Australia will be forgotten.

A *exits.* **B** *prepares, checking clothes, make up, etc. Upright, rigid, purposeful, precise.*

B Who's in charge? We all are. And oh so smug, so

know it all. Who's in charge? I was. Wanted to be. We
need to organise, collectivise, network. To do what?
Nurture? (*Laugh.*) In history women were goddesses, they
had the power. Oh for fuck's sake! That is indicative of the
patriarchal culture seeping into your psyche. If I smash
your face in will that be indicative of patriarchal seepage or
of an intelligent person who's had enough of wishy-washy
wank? Women do not need to express aggression, they can
communicate, they have an inbuilt empathy with their
sisters, we are all on the same side, we all want the same
thing, we are all one. Are you trying to limit me, are you
trying to shackle me, are you trying to control me? Yes
probably. And you said person, you always said person,
refused to acknowledge femininity, masculinity or pronouns
of any description. You were lying too, to begin with. Why
did you come? I was curious. Lonely, depressed, miserable,
but probably more honest than the rest of us, more honest
than me. (*Pause.*) But I've got it now, got what I wanted, I
want you. And the rest, the others still struggling, the ones
without middle-class ideals? You've got to fight for it, it's
not easy, and if that means slapping on the lipstick and
accentuating the sexuality whilst at the same time keeping a
stiff upper lip, but stiffened into a provocative pout, and a
ramrod straight emotionless back, which incidentally
accentuates the breasts, seductively poured into a Gossard
Wonderbra, and a skin so thick a rhinoceros would bounce
off it, whilst at the same time marvelling at the softness and
beauty of the skin tones attentively enhanced by sunbed
shops and Laboratoire Garnier, well so be it. It's what we
fought for and won. You lost, I'm sure you lost, you were
too . . . too romantic, too insular, too . . . poor. I do it all, I
have it all and it isn't enough, it's not what I wanted. I
wanted . . . wanted . . . Want to prove you wrong, want
you to prove me wrong. Want you to say 'no that's not
really what we wanted, we were just young and foolish and
it only seems tangible in retrospect.' You do not need to
grow your own vegetables in order to survive. If you do
not you become a vegetable yourself. Well then I shall
become a very rich and very comfortable vegetable. Well

fuck you then. Fuck me then. Please. (*Pause.*) My God what a failure. A whinging, whining, failure. All this, look at it, you think this amounts to something, do you? You think this is worth something? My God, have you been fooled or what?

A *slouches on.*

B   You came.

A   I was curious.

B   Curiosity killed the cat.

A   Better to be a cat than a bitch.

B   Oh don't start.

A   What?

B   You're starting already.

A   I'm not.

B   You haven't even taken your coat off and you're starting.

A   I'm not starting.

B   You are, you called me a bitch.

A   I did not.

B   You did, you said better to be a cat than a bitch.

A   You said curiosity killed the cat.

B   So?

A   So? I answered.

B   By calling me a bitch.

A   No, not unless you were calling me a cat.

B   That was an expression.

A   That was an answer.

B   A bitchy answer.

A   Now you're calling me a bitch.

B   Only because you started.

A   I didn't start, I wasn't starting.

B   You started before you even got through the door.

A   I wasn't starting.

B   Before you even took your coat off.

A   I wasn't starting, I don't do that any more.

B   What do you mean, you don't do that any more, you've always done, always started, started at the drop of a hat.

A   Not any more, I'm too old now.

B   Started already, before even 'how are you'.

A   Oh shut up, I didn't come here to argue!

Pause.

(*To audience.*) When I was seven this brat came to live with us. She was my cousin. Blonde, pretty, dolly-clutching, goody-goody, yeuk. Everything I hated, a girly girl that everyone adored and felt sorry for and said 'ah isn't she cute'. I hated her.

B   You were jealous.

A   Jealous? Of what? Of a brat who walked as though she was a ballerina even though she was only seven? Of a goody-goody who helped her auntie around the house and was SO well-behaved, SO amenable it made you puke? Who'd sit on uncle's knee, still clutching her stupid dolly, while he read pathetic happy-ever-after fairy stories that she believed and liked and wanted more and more of? Till finally she decided she was going to be a princess just like Andy Pandy.

B   You believed Andy Pandy was a girl too.

A   Yeah, well, only because boys wouldn't wear such

stupid clothes, but I never thought she was a princess.

B   He.

A   He was a princess.

B (*to audience*)   Her mum had always wanted a pretty daughter, a dainty daughter, one who didn't look stupid in pink.

A   And she, Dolly Daisy, fitted the bill. I had my whole life ruined.

B   Not my fault, I didn't come into your life with that express intention.

A   My whole territory invaded.

B   We shared a bedroom. And as I recall we used to giggle and play together quite a lot, when her other little rat-pack friends weren't around.

A   I never realised till she turned up quite how ugly and rebellious I was.

B   You loved it.

A   I loved it. I loved our tent.

B   Our tent. A blanket over the clothes'-line.

A   All enclosed.

B   A secret place.

A   Private.

B   A magical world.

A   Huddled together.

B   Silent.

A   To speak would have broken the spell.

Pause.

B   So you weren't starting then?

A   Not intentionally no.

B   So why did you come?

A   I was curious.

B   Curiosity killed the . . .

A   Oh for God's sake don't start again! You asked me to come.

B   I wanted your support.

A   Why, I've never supported you before?

B   Oh you did. Funnily enough you did.

A   Well I suppose hatred can give you energy.

B   Hatred's too strong a word, but yes something like that. (*To audience.*) I had to adapt and defer to this moody, bossy, unpredictable madam.

A   Don't call me a madam.

B   No of course, she was a tomboy, Little Miss Anarchist – oh the romance of it all, scraggy knees and tree climbing, how pathetic!

A   As opposed to clutching a dolly to your undeveloped bosom, so much more adventurous.

B   That was my security, it reminded me of my mother.

A   Oh well if a dolly reminds you of your mother how could you have grown up any differently. Dollies, women, women, dollies, we might as well stop right now, case closed.

B   Have you any idea what it's like to grow up in someone else's house from the age of seven?

A   No.

B   No. Well shut up then, I'm talking about security not political symbolism.

A   Whoo!

B   She was a moody, bossy, unpredictable MADAM. BUT

she was also energetic and boisterous and I envied that, I wanted to be like her, I wanted to do the things that she did but half of me was scared to try and fail and the other half was scared to try and become better than her. In the end I simply learned to pour scorn on everything she did and at the same time suck up to her mum and dad.

A I could not suck the way she sucked. In the end I didn't even want to.

Pause.

B Not wearing black then?

A Brown boots, he wore brown boots.

B What?

A Brown boots. An old monologue about criticising what a person wears at funerals.

B I wasn't criticising.

A Did you expect me to buy a new outfit?

B Of course not.

A Did you think I'd shave my legs, wax my bikini line, make a special trip to the hairdressers, replenish my make-up bag, buy a new funereal perfume?

B No.

A Did you?

B Did I what?

A Did you buy a new outfit, shave your legs, wax your bikini line, make a special trip to the hairdressers, replenish your make-up bag, and buy a new funereal perfume?

B You're starting again.

A Just making polite conversation.

B Well thank you for being polite.

A You're welcome.

B   Not at all.

A   More tea, vicar?

B   A glass of water would be sufficient.

A   No trouble.

B   No trouble at all.

Extend to comedic well-worn routine.

A   Back straight.

B   Don't talk out of turn.

A   Don't do that, dear.

B   Don't say that, it's rude.

A *and* **B**   And never, never, never, nice girls don't.

A *and* **B**   Curtsey, curtsey, knees together, don't slouch, act like a lady. (*Sing.*) Sisters, sisters . . .

A   Let's have a face pack.

B   Let's shave our legs.

A   Look at her thighs.

B   God, what a slag.

A   Let's go dancing.

B   Let's stay home.

A   Let's tell secrets.

B   Let's giggle about sex.

A   Let's argue.

B   Let's fight.

A *and* **B**   Are you two going to tidy your bedroom or what?

A (*breaking off*)   God did we really use to do that?

B   We were only twelve.

A   How embarrassing.

B   You made up the steps.

A   Shuttup!

B   And the words.

A   Shuttup!! (*To audience.*) Life made no sense to me and being a girl made even less. There was something depressing about it all but I could never put my finger on it.

B   You thought too much. You needed a boyfriend.

A   My mum seemed OK but there was a sadness in her eyes, a look of defeat. She had an intelligence that she dismissed as worthless.

B   You don't need intelligence to get a boyfriend, but padding the bra helps.

A   She felt that pulling your shoulders back and not biting your nails was somehow important to life where argument wasn't.

B   And they love it if you listen attentively and pretend they're intelligent.

A   Inequality didn't matter as much as having a clean house and polite children. The greatest thing my mother could give her family was puddings. Her mum on the other hand . . .

B   Oh here we go.

A   Her mum was swanning around Europe and doing something frightfully glamorous with a long cigarette holder, my mum of course didn't approve but at the same time . . .

B   She was jealous.

A   Jealous as hell.

B   Not jealous of all of it.

A   Jealous of some of it.

B Which bits?

A The freedom bits.

B The independent bits.

A So we both became jealous of those bits.

B Whatever they were.

A We didn't want to end up like my mum anyway.

B Neither of us.

A Not that we wanted to end up like her mum.

B Well, maybe the end but not the means.

A Perhaps something in between.

B If that was possible.

A That was the idea. So I got the freedom to wallow around in chicken shit.

B And I got the independence to employ a cleaner.

A And we thought we wanted the same things.

B We probably do.

Pause.

A But you did though, didn't you? You did buy a new outfit, shave your legs, wax your bikini line, make a special trip to the hairdressers, replenish your make-up bag, and buy a new funereal perfume.

B I do not have to wax my bikini line, I'm blonde . . .

A Whohoo! That's all right then. And what about the rest?

B You have to make an effort.

A It is a special occasion after all.

B You can't just turn up any old how.

A Dressing-gown and slippers.

B It's a mark of respect.

A Mark of position.

B Mark of dignity.

A And you might catch a man, you never know.

B You're starting.

A Just trying to give you energy.

B You don't do that any more, remember?

A That's right, I'm too old now.

B Too old?

A I'm thirty-nine. Practically forty.

B Life begins at forty.

A That's what they say.

B Do you believe them?

A Can't say I do necessarily.

B It's probably because, generally that's when the kids leave home.

A It'll be interesting to see a three-year-old making their way in the world.

B You've got a three-year-old?

A No two.

B Two three-year-olds?

A No one two-year-old.

B One two-year-old and one three-year-old?

A No one.

B No one?

A No one.

B No one? Nobody in the whole world?

A I've always got you.

B Oh well, let the world crash about our ears.

A We used to believe that.

B You did. (*To audience.*) Jealous, I'm not jealous, I never wanted kids, not particularly. Women have choices nowadays.

A Hobson's choices.

B No, definite choices. Definite choices when it comes to breeding anyway. Why did she of all people choose to breed, she's not the type, she's . . . well she's Little Miss Anarchist.

A Do anarchists not have children? Do we not try to breed little anarchists to fight the good fight? Are we not like Catholics trying to take over the world if not by fighting then by sheer volume of offspring? If you marginalise us do we not multiply? If you prick us do we not breed?

B You always said you weren't that female.

A Do people not breed? Is the breeding process something to do with semen and lipstick?

B Boy or girl?

A Which one? This or the other?

B You're having another?

A Isn't it obvious?

B I just thought you'd let yourself go.

A Can't let yourself go when you never got it together in the first place.

B I meant fat, thought you were getting fat.

A Am I supposed to be insulted?

B Probably not, nothing can insult you when it comes to appearance, can it? But then again pregnancy may not become a person of genderless beliefs.

A   Could be a beer gut.

B   Boy or girl?

A   Well, since I'm drinking Bud, it must be a boy gut . . .

B   The other one?

A   Does it make a difference?

B   It would be nice to know, just out of idle curiosity.

A   Well since you're so desperate to know it's a girl.

B   Oh lovely. Is she pretty?

A   Six days old I dressed her in blue, just happened to be blue, and comments were 'Oh what a good strong boy!' 'It's a girl actually.' 'Oh isn't she pretty, isn't she sweet.' Six days old – it's never too early to condition.

B   You're still paranoid about gender then.

A   Of course, stereotyping and pigeonholing are still crimes against humanity in my book.

B   Haven't changed then?

A   Should I have done?

B   Thought you might have by now.

A   Oh because feminism's been fought and won.

B   No, because you're a mother now, thought motherhood might have changed you.

A   Not because you're allowed a career now?

B   Because if motherhood doesn't change you what will?

A   The only thing motherhood changes is sleeping patterns and a stronger conviction that the world is truly fucked, apart from that why should anything?

B   Because you're wrong.

A   Wrong for you.

B Wrong for everybody.

A And you're right, are you?

B More acceptable.

A To who? More acceptable to who? Who accepts a person who sees her own mother's funeral as simply an opportunity to go out and buy some overpriced cocktail dress with matching accessories and spend a day getting pampered in a beauty salon?

B Way below the belt.

A True but enjoyed saying it.

B If it gives me confidence, gives me strength, gives me a sense of who I am at a time of confusion and complicated emotions, why should that be wrong? And anyway look smart or look a mess what's the difference apart from the fact that you think your mother's worth dressing up for. I don't think now is the time for politics, do you? (*Pause.*) I always thought I would be the one to have children, I was always the more feminine, the more womanly. And I can certainly afford the nanny.

A Oh well, breed away then, if you can afford the nanny well what's stopping you?

B Miscarriages mainly. (*Pause.*) I dress up, I look good, I spend time on myself because there doesn't seem to be anything else. I've had lovers, even tried a husband once, but that was probably just a novelty, some bizarre notion of being wanted.

A You were wanted, my parents wanted you, I wanted you. Maybe you just didn't want them. My mum still complains that you never phone, never make contact.

B Sometimes it feels too late, sometimes you just lose contact, feeling.

A We had feelings for each other once.

B I had feelings for her, once, I'm not sure what kind of feelings they were. I have feelings for my mother, I must have, she's my mother. And my aunt and uncle? I loved them I think, once. But . . . I am grieving, I have grieved.

A I'm sure you have.

B I mean about my mother, that other thing was just . . . not meant. I don't care, doesn't bother me, kids are messy things anyway and besides women have choices nowadays.

A Hobson's choices.

B And I simply wouldn't have had the time, too busy, and who wants nannies crawling all over your house, going through your drawers and invading your space.

A I had a cousin who did that once.

B So, whether I choose to pamper myself in a beauty salon or not is irrelevant. I have grieved. In my own way. Surely you approve of that?

A Do whatever you want to do, it's your mother.

B *at first appears upset to fool* **A**, *then a big, over the top pastiche of various ways of mourning – i.e. screaming and tearing hair, falling to knees in quiet shock, struck dumb and fainting etc.*

B How was that?

A Tragic.

B My mother married young.

A Fornicated young.

B She . . .

A Never married.

B Made a mistake. She was a dancer, there were opportunities, do I blame her?

A Yes.

B No. Should I? No. It wasn't meant to be for long, short-term contract. But when you're successful, when you have talent, well, you get better offers, longer offers. If God gives you a talent the worst thing to do is squander it. Is it better to do the best for yourself and your child or to spend your child's life growing in resentment and frustration? And anyway we caught up, eventually, I believe we were closer for it, appreciated each other much more because of the difficulties we overcame and the sacrifices we made.

A   Her mother was a selfish cow who did exactly what she wanted to do, most of it involving men. Definition of a dancer, one who can't keep her legs together long enough to debate whether opening them would be a good idea or not.

B   That's not true.

A   If you say so.

B   She was a good dancer, successful, went from strength to strength.

A   Is that what they're calling it nowadays?

B   You cannot turn down opportunities if opportunities present themselves, we all only have one life.

A   And we have to prioritise, work out what's most important to us, discard the thing or person that's not, and if that means just dumping your daughter on your sister's doorstep then so be it.

B   Shut up, don't start.

A   Nah you're right, it's too early and way below the belt.

Pause.

B   I don't think I know how to.

A   How to what?

B   How to grieve.

A   Fair enough.

B   It all feels quite strange.

A Well, I suppose you didn't know her too well.

B Oh, I know her all right, I've become her.

A You mean a tart?

B You're doing it again!

A I can't help it.

B She was not a tart.

A OK, if you insist, I don't care either way.

B And your mother was so good, was she?

A I think so, don't you?

B Well, you've changed your tune, what happened to all the scorn you'd heap on the downtrodden, second-class housewife who'll do anything for a quiet life except fight for her rights.

A Yeah I think I'm becoming that.

B Oh yeah, 'Earth Mother' with your two-year-old and another on the way.

A Yes I'm just a housewife and mother, feminism has given me that much.

B So feminism put the 'just' in housewife.

A Either that or become 'just' another man.

B Feminism gave you choices.

A Hobson's choices.

B Real choices.

A Hey ho the revolution.

B And what happened to yours?

A My what?

B Your revolution.

A I couldn't afford the nanny. Did you invite me to talk about feminism?

B No.

A What is it? Twenty-five/thirty years of the stuff? And what have you changed? What's changed about you? You've been holding your stomach in since I got here.

B No I haven't.

A Have, look at you!

B I have not got a stomach, I work out!

A What's the difference? Working out – holding your stomach in – it's all the same. You're still not allowed to have a stomach.

B It's not that. I choose to look good because it's healthy and it makes me feel good.

A Bollocks! You're just using your prettiness and feminine charm to make your way in the world – same as ever.

B Ha I don't need to, I use my business acumen.

A In jeans and a T-shirt? I don't think so.

B I don't wear jeans and a T-shirt.

A Exactly why not? Why do you have to tart yourself up? Are your suspenders holding up your brains? When there's a woman on the telly who looks as scruffy as Bob Geldof, then let's discuss feminism, shall we, sister? But until then, what are you going to do when it all starts sagging? Oops no, it has, hasn't it, look at those wrinkles! Look at your face. How did you get to be so old? What we need is some youth rejuvenating face cream with action liposomes, Laboratoire Garnier – Le Jardin – with a dry weave top sheet, I bet you've got some . . .

*Rummages through **B**'s make-up bag.*

In fact a dry weave top sheet on your face may improve matters. (*Finds a jar.*) Yes I knew you would . . . look, it says 'anti-wrinkle' – doesn't work, does it? My placenta's in this, you know. They put human placenta in this, my two-year-old's placenta is probably on your face even as we speak. (*Hand over face.*) Do I look younger? Yeah you've got a face like a foetus, so much younger . . .

B (*heavily ironic*) I've also done psychotherapy, hypnotherapy, behaviour therapy, group therapy, aromatheropy, Prozac, massage, meditation, tai chi, isolation tanks, aerobics and colonic irrigation . . .

A   Colonic irrigation? How the hell does someone get the idea to have colonic irrigation? And why? Did you wake up in the morning and say 'Oh I feel so . . . so . . . so full of shit, I think I'll go to a clinic and have somebody shove a hosepipe up my bum, squirt some water up me and see what comes out – ooh look, a piece of lettuce I ate in 1967, I feel so much better now!'

B   'What we need to do is turn our back on society, buy up little plots of land and grow our own vegetables, be self sufficient then we'll all be in paradise.'

A   My time will come.

B   Probably with the next messiah.

A   Nah because the next messiah would want to be in charge, and where I live . . .

A *and* **B**   We all are.

B   Oh well feminism gave you something at least.

A   Nothing to do with feminism, everything to do with equality, we've got men in our group.

B   Obviously and you've been fucking at least one of them.

A   Oh at least. Would you like a list? Because unlike some people, I don't fall apart every time a man sticks his cock in me.

B   Meaning?

A   You know what I mean.

B   No I don't, I have absolutely no problems with men.

A   Must have been practising then because last time I saw you with one you were falling apart at the seams . . .

B   I was only fifteen for God's sakes! His name was Tim and I was mad about him. He was twenty and exciting, he had a car, and money and a wealth of experience and a sexual appetite that I willingly succumbed to.

A   I was hoping that she might get pregnant, that would give my mother the vapours, wouldn't be the blue-eyed girl then, would she?

B   Then he dumped me.

A   Shouldn't have lowered yourself in the first place.

B   I was devastated.

A   Anybody's who's anybody knows boys are stupid.

B   I felt my world had collapsed.

A   Not that I'd ever had a boyfriend.

B   Felt suicidal.

A   Not that I wanted one.

B   No reason for living.

A   But it would've been nice to be asked.

B   And my aunt and uncle were out for the evening, leaving just the two of us and I was crying in the bathroom and I looked such a mess and I had a cold on top of everything and I was wearing my uncle's big clumpy dressing-gown because it had a secure feeling about it.

A   We all wore my dad's big clumpy dressing-gown whenever any of us felt a bit low – smelt of nicotine, sweat and beer, lovely.

B   And I came down to make a cup of tea and I spilt it and I cried again because it was the last straw and she kissed me.

A　I kissed her. She looked so awful she looked beautiful.

B　She kissed me so lovingly, so softly.

A　It was a great dressing-gown.

B　And . . .

A　And?

B　And.

A　Since seven our bodies developing at roughly the same rate.

B　Strange feelings, urges.

A　A compulsion.

B　To do something sexual.

A　Without realising it was sexual.

B　We became secret friends.

A　We both knew how to touch each other to create an electric charge.

B　Because we were both suffering from the same confusion.

A　And experimentation became an obsession.

B　A secret passion.

A　Because although this wasn't sex,

B　Sex was something to do with boys.

A　And there were no boys present.

B　It was something private.

A　Something personal between the two of us. A secret language.

B　Secret communication.

A　To speak would have broken the spell.

B　Like adolescent sorcery and witchcraft.

A   And then came sex.

B   This was how sex was supposed to be.

A   I felt wanted, beautiful, I knew what I was doing.

B   I was losing control.

A   And then Australia. Her mother marrying, setting up a new life, some new au pair agency business, wanting her, the sudden apple of her eye, 'Come with us,' she said, 'let me be a real mother now.' And Dolly Daisy went. And I wanted nothing else, I needed nothing else, only records to make love by and her. She went to Australia and by sixteen I was out of the game.

B   You weren't out of the game.

A   Wasn't I?

B   I came back.

A   I'm not going to flatter myself to think you came back because of me.

B   Maybe I did maybe I didn't.

A   Maybe you came back because your mother didn't want you after all?

B   Did I tell you I finally bought the Porsche?

A   How pointless. Did she or didn't she?

B   Maybe my mother just didn't want you any more. Totally useless and impractical of course, the Porsche, but at least it gave me the opportunity to socialise with all the people who feel having a Porsche is a talking point.

A   This is pointless, stop it – What do you mean . . . ?

B   I bet you don't even own a microwave, do you?

A   No.

B   No, because you were never prepared to work for one.

A   It was never a driving ambition no. What do you

mean, your mother didn't want me any more?

B Told you often enough. Told you ages ago. Would you listen? Would you heck. I said turn the trivial into an art form, make it serious, turn it into the most important part of your life I said, people do, other people, people who are determined to see a point in everything, even a humble microwave – make it the best, the most up to the minute, the latest, greatest most wonderful microwave in the world. Of course I do have the best microwave in the world.

A Your mother didn't want me?

B I became you, became Little Miss Anarchist.

A You became me?

B Cut off my hair, let myself go, scragged around in jeans, tried to be boyish, surly, aggressive, politics, tried to think 'politics', what's wrong, what makes me angry? My mother. I hated her, hated her. Selfish, moody, neurotic, cow. Fought like a hard-faced bitch with anybody and everybody over the slightest thing, then wanted me to mother her like a baby, wanted me to reassure her, that I loved her, that I cared about her, that somebody cared about her, that she was still attractive, that she still had it all, money, men, looks and me. And I spat in her eye, wanted to spit in her eye, spit like you spat, because what about me? Did she care about me? At all? Her husband she used, she didn't love him, couldn't love him, didn't know how, didn't know how to love anyone, so she just used him to set up the business, used his money, used his knowledge, used his contacts, then divorce, quick clean, move on, no regrets, no feelings. No feelings, she had no feelings. I despised her, I saw in her what you see in me, greed and materialism. And that's where you went wrong. You see, had you just got yourself something, something to show off about, just to show you meant business, just to show that you were better than them, they would have taken you seriously then, would've listened to you, seen that you had something to offer. But what are you offering? Nothing, you're impressing nobody. They can't even say

'She's completely off her rocker but at least she's got a decent microwave.' Me, I can impress. People listen, people take note. I've got property, I've bought land, lots of it. I own practically a whole village in Kent, so people listen to me.

A   Worth getting a good microwave then.

B   We all need money.

A   What for?

B   To show everybody we've got some.

A   Oh.

B   See, there's a point to everything when you're competing.

A   Competing for what?

B   To prove there's a point.

A   But there isn't one, is there? There is no fucking point.

B   That's why you came, isn't it? Weren't curious at all, just wanted to gloat, wanted to rub my nose in it – 'Look at her fancy clothes and a Porsche, who does she think she is? Nobody as usual.' That's why you're here, isn't it? To say 'Thirty-nine, approaching forty and what's she got to show for it? Nothing. Nothing all crammed into a miracle of technology, state of the art, fucking microwave fucking Porsche.' Isn't it? Isn't it?

A   Well, no actually.

B   Go on say it, say what you're supposd to say, say 'My God what a failure. A whinging, whining, failure. All this, look at it, you think this amounts to something, do you? You think this is worth something? My God, have you been fooled or what?'

B *starts aggressively taking clothes off.*

A   I never realised being rich could be so depressing.

B   Don't laugh. Don't you bloody laugh at me!

A   Who's laughing?

B   You are. Sitting there smug in the knowledge that you never tried to better yourself because you knew it wouldn't work, knew it wasn't what I wanted. Who's in charge?

A   We all are.

B   Yeah. Happy now?

A   Not particularly.

B   Well, do it then.

A   Do what?

B   Do what you came for. Argue, shout, get overheated, tell me I'm a vegetable, go on, knock me sideways, make me feel like shit and then kiss me and tell me how it can be better.

A   I don't know how to any more.

B   Well then I'm buggered.

A (*to audience*)   I shouldn't have come, I half thought it might be a mistake, but now I'm sure of it. A Porsche for fuck's sake, am I supposed to be impressed? And don't ask me to offer an alternative because I lost a long time ago. Lost direction, lost my energy, lost the will to fight – never knew what I was fighting for. Only ever knew what I didn't want, could never say what I did want, except to go away somewhere else somewhere away from this crap world and this crap society with its microwaves and colonic irrigation and bikini lines.

B   But your commune?

A   Commune? Yeah right, commune. Nah, we had a meeting, lasted four days. We're a co-operative now. A co-operative. A supplier of organically grown fruit and vegetables to a middle-class elite who can afford to pay over the odds to eat politically correct cabbages.

B   But turning your back on society and creating your own non-materialistic, self-sufficient world where everybody is encouraged to realise their own potential and each person is of equal importance in contributing to the group well-being of an alternative, self-supporting community of like-minded individuals?

A You remembered.

B How could I forget.

A I had. No we're now just a small business, a cottage industry, we're even supplying Sainsbury's – we even pay tax, that's how radical we are.

B Perhaps you need money to be self-sufficient?

A Lots and lots and lots of it.

Both laugh. **A** *picks up black trousers and T-shirt from her chair.*

A What're these?

B Funereal garments.

A Funereal garments? Are these supposed to be for me?

B Thought you might want them.

A Of course because you never know, I might turn up like Ronald McDonald. Well, they won't fit. See I've got child-bearing hips now – my hips have expanded to fit me better . . . course my tampon keeps falling out but there you go . . . (*Throws them to* **B**.) You wear them.

B *puts them on.*

B Why did you leave?

A It was getting out of hand.

B I don't want to be alone when I die.

A She wasn't alone, her employees were concerned.

B She'd been dead all weekend.

A So? Some people are dead for weeks, months, it's only when the neighbours report a funny smell that anybody notices.

B You won't die like that, will you?

A Doubt it.

B I might.

A I don't think you'll care, you'll be dead.

B You've got your farm, your friends, your family. I want to be you. Is this because of my mother? Is it? Is this grief? Or am I really stuck? Am I really stuck with this pretence till I die, like she stuck with her pretence, because it was a pretence, it was all pretence, right down to her nail polish and hair colouring. I don't even think she liked me, let alone loved.

A That's not true necessarily.

B Isn't it?

A She took you to Australia.

B Did she?

A Didn't she?

B Oh she tried, I'm not saying she didn't try. She told me, it's what she worked for, setting up the agency, becoming respectable, having enough money to afford to care for me.

A My mother had nothing and she cared for you.

B I know.

A Do you know how she felt when you left? Do you know how my dad felt? Do you know how I felt listening to them talk about you all the time? It was all you, you, you. They hadn't a clue what I was going to do with my life, but certainly didn't think it was anything to get excited about, it would be something embarrassing probably, something they'd deplore, like saving whales or something. God, I wanted to blow the whole fucking thing up!

B Did you ever want to be me?

A Too fucking right I did, I was crazy about you, nuts

about you. (*To audience.*) I prayed, every night I prayed to God for her to come back, which was embarrassing because I was an atheist at the time. And then the pissy thing was she did come back, back from Australia, back from down under. Who's in charge?

B We all are.

A God, she annoyed me then. The feminist boom was a life-saver.

B A miracle.

A Perfect timing.

B The hand of fate.

A Changed my life.

B Well, it did change my life. I came back to England in 1980, set up my own business, using the Assets you Need to be Successful. I was twenty-four. My mother I used, I didn't love her, couldn't love her, didn't know how, didn't know how to love anyone, so I just used her to set up the business, used her money, used her knowledge, used her contacts, then separation, quick clean, move on, no regrets, no feelings. No feelings, she had no feelings, I had no feelings. And I got in touch. It was now on my turf, my terms. The flat in London was my flat, my friends, it was going to be my time.

A Oh you think so, do you?

B I just thought you'd be interested, this is going to be a revolution.

A Well, I like a good revolution, who's in charge?

B We all are.

A What does that mean?

B Means we all agree to go along with the consensus.

A Doesn't sound like much of a revolution to me.

B Be patient, the world's going to change.

A Are you sure?

B The patriarchal hierarchy will topple and be replaced by a fairer, more equitable society.

A Will every man, woman and child be given due respect and be allowed to fulfil their potential?

B Of course and women will end up on top.

A On top of what? The wardrobe?

B On top of whoever's underneath. (*To audience.*) And I could impress. Oh could I impress. 'Lesbianism is a political statement.' Yes. Been there, done it. Done it! Yes, sisters, I'm there, I'm with you, I get the point. A political statement, yes! You and me at fifteen, all those years ago, we were a political statement!

A Oh I am creaming my jeans, I'm sliding off my chair, my juice is on the loose. I've never felt so horny in all my life. Come back to my place and let's be a political statement. If we orgasm we can call it a manifesto. Did you really just see us as a political statement?

B Of course not, I was just trying to curry favour with our friends.

A Your friends.

B And I knew it wound you up, irritated you. If I didn't care would I have found you again? Would I have got you involved?

A Oh I believed in feminism to begin with.

B No you didn't.

A No you're right I believed in anarchy. I didn't want equality I wanted Utopia. Do you really want a revolution? Really? Land. Think about it. A farm, lots of land in Wales or Norfolk or somewhere. Get a group of people, men and women, pool our resources, buy it. Better still, you buy it. Sell your business. You won't need it, an employment agency's really crap anyway, who needs that? That's a stupid job. Anyway we won't need employment, won't need money, won't need men, or women or stupid divisions like that, just need people. People with a human spirit. People who don't give a stuff about the priorities of this inhuman society.

B Patriarchal society.

A Materialistic society.

B It's patriarchal in communist countries too.

A Of course it is, because it's all economics, that's my point, the whole world's based on money. And money's inhuman, it segregates and separates people. Money created lipstick and push-up bras to segregate women, and money created stiff upper lips and ramrod straight emotionless backs to segregate men. Your women's movement won't get anywhere without tackling the economics of it all.

B The women's movement IS tackling economics, economic equality. We need to organize, collectivise, network.

A To do what? Nurture? Because what are you going to do with the kids? Kids are a burden till they are economically viable for this shitty society. But farming, growing crops and being self-sufficient, everybody all together with their kids, men and women, together – like monkeys. We could be like monkeys. Monkeys aren't fucked up, monkeys don't need money, female monkeys aren't collectivising and networking!

B Women don't want to be monkeys. Nobody wants to be a monkey . . .

A I do.

B In history women were goddesses they had the power.

A Oh for fuck's sakes, goddesses. Diaphanous women waltzing around with urns on their shoulders. So radical!

B That is indicative of the patriarchal culture seeping into your psyche.

A If I smash your face in will that be indicative of patriarchal seepage or of an intelligent person who's had enough of wishy-washy women's wank? (*To audience.*) I just wanted to be with her, all the time, constantly, I had an all consuming passion, I wanted to destroy everything and have just the two of us survive. Just you, me and a row of marrows.

B And the other woman?

A What other woman?

B (*to audience*) We used to all meet up in a gay bar, there were men but they didn't bother us.

A Too busy going down on each other in the toilets.

B I was in the thick of things.

A Ha!

B Popular, entertaining. I was on the cutting edge – a straight woman having a lesbian relationship because it was a political statement.

A They all fancied me, they were just jealous because you were the one who had me, nothing political at all.

B So there I was holding court, the centre of things, speaking from experience, speaking from the perspective of a woman who knows both sides and so knows the problem inside and out. Talking politics and sisterhood. Spouting how two women have loving, caring, sharing relationships as opposed to men having sex. Women developing empathy with each other while men seek instant gratification. Two women emotionally linked as opposed to men just sticking it in and jerking off – and where was she? While all our friends were listening to this diatribe? Where was she?

A Going down on some woman in the toilets.

B Going down on some woman in the toilets.

A My turn to go down under I think. It was just sex. It was a joke.

B   Wasn't a joke. You'd done it before, everybody knew you'd done it before, everybody, except me, knew, knew what a fool I was.

A   Well you deserved it, you were a hypocrite, if for one moment I thought that what you were spouting was in any way connected to the way we were living I might have let you get away with it. But it wasn't, you were just a liar, not happy with me, had to invent me, invent a life with me to look good in front of your friends. You were trying to be so fucking political, so right on, women this, women that, let's all be goddesses, let's refuse to argue, let's show the patriarchal society how we can all sit in a circle and be at one with our wombs, for Christ's sakes. I wanted to kick your feminist credentials down your throat and have you choke on them.

B   It was the only time in my life that I felt I belonged, that I wasn't just muscling in, that people actually liked me, wanted me, welcomed me in to the centre of things. And you just ensured that they laughed at me, I was their evening's entertainment, a laughing stock. You never understood.

A   No you never understood. I'd have much rather it was you in that toilet, everybody could have watched and really applauded you then.

B   Don't be disgusting, I wouldn't have lowered myself.

A   No, I'd be the one going down.

B *goes to hit* **A** *but thinks better of it.*

A   Sorry was I turning you on? (*To audience.*) She liked sex. Sex that was raw and rough and angry, she wanted to be humiliated, kicked in the teeth and then fucked, fucked with a vengeance, she wanted her nose rubbed in it, wanted me to take her down, way down to the depths of self-loathing because it was the only way she could feel, only way she felt about herself, only way she could make contact with herself. We lived on top of each other and stifled and suffocated till sometimes our arguments and fights turned to hatred, but we became ourselves then, our true animal selves, sweating and snarling and loving each other with a passion that was so overwhelming, so consuming we didn't care what we looked like, how we appeared to each other, didn't care who was me and who was her, we were entwined with each other totally, wallowing in mud while the world disintegrated around us, and it all came from down here, way, way down deep inside us, moaning and raging and wanting to burst, burst out of us in the true spirit of what? what was it? femininity? humanity? hatred? rage? jealousy . . .

B She fucked anybody. Slagged around with anybody because it was the only way of getting attention. Set herself up as some sort of radical thinker, pioneer revolutionary, people would write books about her, see her in centuries to come as the saviour of mankind – oh yeah right, if anybody bothered to listen to her at all. And did they? Did they listen to you? Did they want to know about your grand plans, your earth shattering schemes? No. So you had to fuck instead, as a joke. Be the joker in the pack, the court jester because nobody would take you seriously would they, nobody gave a toss about what you thought or what you said, just so long as it was funny. All you could be was funny. Big deal.

A We were both funny, Tom and Jerry, Laurel and Hardy, Cain and bloody Abel.

B You used to complain that boys wouldn't listen to you when we were young and then there you were and women wouldn't listen to you either, my God the only reason they fucked you was because unlike the boys, it was politically OK for lesbians to be ugly. It was politically OK to fuck a joke!

A *grabs* **B**, *about to hit, then kisses and pushes* **B** *away.*

B Go on do it, do it again!

A *backs off.*

B Want me to fetch a knife?

A   Wish now I'd worn black. (*To audience*.) It's all personal,
deep down. I pretended it was political, I ranted and raved
about revolutions and changing the world and equality in
every form I could think of, but actually it was just
personal and I made it political. I made it all political
because I couldn't stand the idea that anybody, particularly
her, would think I was jealous. I never wanted to be pretty,
I never wanted to be some hot-shot careerist either. But I
didn't want eyes like my mother's eyes, I didn't want to
become obsessed with puddings. I'm thirty-nine,
approaching forty. It doesn't matter any more. I make the
best of it like my mother did, like my dad, I poddle around
on my little market garden with my friends and pretend it
all means something radically political, but it doesn't, just
means we're market gardeners.

B   So. You left.

A   I'm not starting.

B   You left.

A   Yes I left, I meant it.

B   We never discussed you leaving.

A   It was never open for discussion.

B   Everything is open for discussion.

A   I'm not starting.

B   No I am.

A   OK I left, but then again you left first maybe I was
just getting even.

B   You're dragging up Australia again.

A   Too right I am, everything is open for discussion.

B   My mother asked me to join her, at sixteen I was
curious.

A   Curiosity killed the cat.

B   Better to be a cat than a bitch.

A You calling me a bitch?

B Yes I am.

A Why, because I'm calling your mother a slag? A tart, no better than a prostitute, in fact your mother wasn't really a dancer, was she? She was a hostess, we all know that, a hostess, sleeping her way around the bars and cabarets of Europe, opening her legs for materialism, sucking cocks for capitalism – AND, what's interesting is she preferred doing that than having to deal with you. She didn't want you, she'd rather have a cock jammed down her throat – interesting.

B And I preferred being with her than being with you – interesting.

A That's not true.

B Because she never asked me to go.

A Yes she did.

B No I asked her if I could so that I could get away from you.

A No we loved each other then.

B No, you loved me. I just loved the way you squirmed underneath me, loved the way you needed me, were besotted by me. You were so exciting, so frightening, a bossy boots, a scraggy, argumentative, energetic, anarchist right from seven. And I was so stuck, so insecure, so unsure of myself – all our friends were your friends, all our games were your games, all our ideas were your ideas. Oh until we were teenagers, I thought I had you then, because I had the advantage, I had the goods, the necessary abilities to win. Till I was humiliated, dumped, treated with contempt for granting some spotty imbecile a couple of sexual favours, and an abortion thrown in on top, with your mother's collusion, oh you didn't know that, did you? And then the eighties and I was terrified that feminism would be your time, that you'd take over, that you'd gain control through revolution and equality for uglies. But turned out it was easy, it was so easy.

A Of course it was easy, course it was easy. Because feminism was just about becoming like your mother. And you have become her, exactly the same as her, like mother like daughter.

B Not so.

A What's changed?

B Equality.

A Oh please don't make me laugh, you're still having to wear lipstick to emphasise the colour of your cunt, you're still flaunting your sexuality in order to acquire a Porsche, the only thing that's changed is whether you choose to suck dick or kiss arse for fuck's sakes.

B God, you make me so sick I could hit you.

A Good, it'll stop me from having to hit you.

B You have done absolutely nothing with your life, you sit there like a beached whale talking about politics and how we should all opt out and blow the system up and grow vegetables because you're too scared to dip a toe in the water, too scared to try and be halfway better than the next person because you might fail, you're terrified of failing, terrified of anybody saying you've made a mistake so you pretend it's political, pretend dressing to impress is somehow flaunting your cunt – you're pathetic.

A At least I'm not a screaming neurotic like you, at least I don't have to run myself ragged buying lots of useless stuff to clutter up my life because I'm desperately trying to fill the void of a hollow existence.

B You've done nothing.

A I've had kids.

B Yeah pure accidents I'll bet.

A Totally meant actually, in fact I'd have bred dozens by now if I hadn't exercised restraint because I'm so fecund it's frightening, unlike someone who can't even manage one.

B   I didn't want one.

A   Well, why try then?

B   Because I'm a woman.

A   Fuck off that's pathetic!

B   I wanted to be a juggling, struggling career woman, I wanted a fashion accessory, I wanted endless discussions about me and my problems coping with a career and kids in the *Guardian* women pages, I wanted to have it all, I wanted to complain about nannies and the difficulties in finding a good one, and I wanted to pour scorn on the best ones because they weren't as good as me, and I wanted to be the perfect feminist who joins the ranks of the patriarchal elite and wields power just as effectively under the guise of equality and revolution, I wanted no time to think, I wanted to be so rushed I had no time for anything especially myself, I wanted to have it all because I can't see the point. Everything in this life is so pointless, everything I do amounts to nothing and there's got to be a point somewhere, I've got to find something and I've got to find it before you do because I love you and I want to know why you left.

A   You know why I left.

B   No I don't.

A   It was obvious, you'd be dead otherwise.

B   It was what I wanted.

A   No it wasn't. What you wanted was triumph, what you wanted was my death.

B (*to audience*)   She was chopping carrots, home-grown . . .

A   You just wanted to drag me down into the hole that you're in.

B   She had an allotment in those days . . .

A   There is a point to your life, it's all about winning.

B   If you were interested in compost her conversations could be riveting.

A   And you want to call that success – no, no you want ME to call that success, you can't stand the fact that I don't.

B   She never cared what people thought.

A   Well shall I? Shall I climb into your hole?

B   We were arguing . . .

A   Shall I show you how bloody easy it is to do what you're supposed to do and call it success?

B   . . . a tent in the country somewhere, our blanket over the clothes'-line . . .

A   To just slot yourself into the mainstream?

B   . . . self-sufficiency, our magical world.

A   And then blame everybody else because you're still not bloody happy?

B   I've never had sex like I had sex with her.

A *starts changing.*

A   Do you know if it hadn't been for you I would probably have been successful by now. Probably have been running myself ragged the way you are.

B   And she was chopping the carrots, arguing.

A   My 'commune' brothers and sisters? All their talk about alternative societies?

B   I said: You do not need to grow your own vegetables in order to survive.

A   Dropping out like hippies, being equal like feminists, being more equal than feminists.

B   She said: If you don't you become a vegetable yourself.

A   Not doing the male thing but actually trying to do the female thing, the seasons and the earth and mother fucking nature.

B   I said: Well then I shall become a very rich and very comfortable vegetable.

A   Should I be mad now that we're SO part of middle-class society that we're even supplying Sainsbury's?

B   She said: Well fuck you then.

A   Should I be mad?

B   I said: Fuck me then.

A   Should I be raging that anything that could make the slightest bit of difference to the world has been changed, weakened, diluted simply to suit the status quo?

B   And the knife goes in – pop. She just turns round and knifes me.

A *stops ranting.*

B   Slicing carrot, slicing me – her favourite vegetable.

A   No. I don't care any more. This stuff doesn't bloody fit . . . I don't care. I'm happy and I don't give a fuck! I can't get into any of your stuff! (*Sudden shout.*) I meant it. I'm not sorry. I meant it. Only honest thing I did. Wanted to get inside, right inside, right inside you, have you be real, have you be honest. (*Pause.*) This stuff doesn't fit.

A *takes black tablecloth and wraps it round her.*

B   What are you doing?

A   I'm wearing black. I'm in mourning for my life.

B   You look pathetic.

A   I haven't finished yet. Got to accessorise . . .

Puts cloth over head – a chador.

Right, I'm ready. I hope it's a religious service. Actually Iran's got the right idea, only trouble is they've only gone halfway. If everybody wore these chadar things, men and women, wow! We could be anybody under here, all of us just black blobs with eyes, all making our way down to the DIY stores on Sunday, we could be anybody, doing anything – and we could shoplift. Just seeing each other's eyes and saying 'I fancy those eyes' then taking them home and what's underneath? Whoo lovely! or Ugly nasty drippy thing! whatever. Could be brilliant – that's what I call a revolution.

B *moves and kisses* **A**. **A** *puts 'chador' round* **B** *while kissing, but eventually breaks off – both stand with just their faces showing through.*

A   Wait a minute, what about Australia?

B   I had to leave, had to get away – you were in charge and I wanted to be.

A   Is that why? Why you left?

B   And you? Why did you leave?

A   It's obvious, you were in charge and I wanted to be.

B   And now?

A   It's too late now.

B   But I practically own a whole village, I'm selling up the business . . .

A   No it's too late.

B   So why did you come?

A   I was curious.

B   Curiosity killed the cat.

A   Didn't it just. (*Pause.*) I'm sorry about your mother's death.

Lights fading.

B   Shall we go to the funeral now?

A   If you're ready.

B   I still don't think I know how to act.

A   See what happens when they chuck dirt on her coffin.

B   It feels so strange.

A   Just keep your eye on my mum, see how she reacts.

B   Is your mum going to be there?

A   Of course, they were sisters, you know.

B   Frightening.

A   Murderous (*Sings.*) sisters, sisters, there were never such psychotic sisters . . .

B   Are we really going like this?

A   Why not? What's the matter would you rather shag instead?

B   Don't start.

A   What?

B   You're starting.

A   I'm not.

B   You are.

A   It was just a joke.

B   Well, it's not funny.

A   OK I was just making polite conversation.

B   Well, thank you for being polite.

A   You're welcome.

B   Not at all.

A   More tea, vicar?

B   A glass of water would be sufficient.

A   No trouble.

B   No trouble at all.

Blackout.

9 780413 712905